LOUD AND CLEAR

Stopping Silent Treatment and Reviving Your Relationship"

Copyright © 2004 by Cheryl T. Long

All rights reserved. No part of this book may be reproduced, distributed, or transmitted in any form or by any means, including photocopying, recording, or other electronic or mechanical methods, without the prior written permission of the author, except in the case of brief quotations embodied in critical reviews and certain other noncommercial uses permitted by copyright law.

ISBN: 9781949807158

Published by Dear Daughters Love Mom

Second Edition

DEDICATION

To all those who have ever felt silenced or alone, This book is dedicated to you.

To the hearts burdened by unspoken words, And the souls searching for light in the shadows, May you find solace, strength, and healing in these stories.

To the seekers of peace who turn to prayer in the quiet of the night,

To those who find comfort in meditation and reflection, And to the faithful who hold onto hope in the midst of pain, This is for you.

To the ones who, despite the silence, choose to love, To the brave who stand firm in their beliefs, Even when the world around them falls into quiet, You are seen, you are valued, and you are never truly alone.

May your faith, in whatever form it takes, Guide you through the darkest of times, And lead you to a place of understanding, Where love speaks louder than silence.

To the resilient souls that refuse to break, And to the spirit of faith that unites us all, This book is a testament to the strength within each of us, And the healing power of faith and connection.

This is for you.

PREFACE

Dear Reader,

The book you hold is more than just a collection of words on paper. It's a beacon of hope, a roadmap to healing, and a testament to the resilience of the human spirit.

I wrote this book because I've been where you are. I've felt the crushing weight of silence, the confusion of trying to navigate a relationship where communication has broken down, and the despair of wondering if things will ever change. But I'm here to tell you change is possible. Healing is possible. And you are stronger than you know.

In these pages, you'll find not only my story but the collective wisdom of countless others who have walked this path. You'll discover practical strategies for dealing with silent treatment, insights into the psychology behind this harmful behavior, and most importantly, tools to reclaim your voice and your power.

This book is for anyone who has ever felt unheard, invisible, or insignificant in their relationship. It's for those who are ready to break the cycle of silence and step into a life of open, honest communication and genuine connection.

As you read, remember you are not alone. Your experiences are valid, your feelings matter, and you deserve to be treated with respect and kindness. My hope is that this book will be a companion on your journey, offering support, guidance, and encouragement every step of the way.

Wording:

- **Trigger Warning:** This book discusses the silent treatment, a form of emotional manipulation. If you have experienced emotional abuse, some parts of this book may be triggering.
- **Content Advisory:** This book explores the negative impacts of the silent treatment in relationships. If you are currently experiencing emotional abuse, you may find the content difficult.

Thank you for having the courage to pick up this book and take the first step towards change. I believe in you, and I'm honored to be a part of your healing journey.

With hope and solidarity,

Cheryl T long

TABLE OF CONTENTS

Introduction: Breaking the Silence 1

Understanding the Silent Treatment 1

The Impact of Silent Treatment 2

Chapter 1 : "The Silent Treatment: A Narcissist's Abusive Partner's Secret Weapon" 6

Understanding the Power Dynamic 6

The Psychology Behind Silent Treatment 9

Chapter 2: "The Many Faces of Silence: Types of Silent Treatment" 14

The Complete Shutdown 14

The Minimal Responder 15

The Selective Silence 16

The Ghosting Silent Treatment 17

The Passive-Aggressive Communicator 18

Chapter 3: "The Silent Wounds: How the Silent Treatment Affects You" 21

It Destroys Your Self-Esteem 21

It Creates Anxiety and Depression 23

It Makes You Doubt Your Perception of Reality 24

It Damages Your Other Relationships 25

It Can Lead to Physical Health Problems 26

It Makes You Lose Your Voice 27

Chapter 4: "Breaking the Silence: Strategies for Dealing with Silent Treatment" 30

Recognize It's Not Your Fault 30

Don't Chase the Silent Partner 31

Set Clear Boundaries 32

Practice Self-Care 32

Keep Communication Open on Your End 33

Seek Professional Help 33

Know Your Limits 34

Chapter 5: "Staying Strong: Maintaining Progress and Handling Setbacks" 36

Celebrate Small Victories 36

Expect and Prepare for Setbacks 37

Keep Learning and Growing 38

Regularly Reassess Your Boundaries 39

Maintain Your Identity Outside the Relationship 40

Practice Ongoing Communication 40

Be Patient with Yourself and Your Partner 41

Chapter 6: "Healing and Growing: Long-Term Strategies for Overcoming Silent Treatment" 44

Rebuild Your Self-Esteem 44

Develop Emotional Intelligence 45

Explore Your Passions 48

Learn About Healthy Relationships 50

Chapter 7: "Drawing Strength from Faith" chapter: 52

Finding Comfort in Spiritual Practices 52

Using Faith as an Anchor in Difficult Times 53

Integrating Faith into Your Healing Journey 54

Balancing Faith and Action 55

Overcoming Faith-Based Challenges 56

Faith and Self-Worth 57

Sharing Your Faith Journey 57

Faith and Future Relationships 58

Personal Stories of Faith and Healing 59

Chapter 8: Reclaiming Your Love Life 63

Understanding the Impact 64

Finding Your Worth 64

Communicating Your Needs 65

Trust and Vulnerability 66

Dating After the Silent Treatment 66

Finding a Supportive Partner 67

Chapter 9: "When Silence Becomes Deafening: Recognizing the Point of No Return" 71

Recognizing the Danger Signs 73

Assessing Your Relationship 74

The Strength of Choosing to Leave 75

When Staying Might Be an Option 76

Moving Forward 77

Chapter 10: "Moving Forward: Navigating Your Path to Long-Term Healing" 79

Personal Growth and Self-Reflection 79

Advanced Healing Strategies 81

Chapter 11: "Living Your Best Life: Integrating Healing Strategies into Daily Life" 95

Creating a Daily Healing Routine 95

Micro-Moments of Self-Compassion 96

Weekly Check-Ins and Reflections 97

Creating a Supportive Environment 98

Balancing Solitude and Connection 99

Chapter 12: "The Long Haul: Sustaining Your Healing Journey" 101

Understanding the Healing Cycle 101

Adapting Your Strategies Over Time 102

Handling Triggers and Flashbacks 103

Maintaining Boundaries in the Long Term 103

Evolving Your Support System 104

Integrating Your Healing into Your Identity 104

Passing It On Using Your Experience to Help Others ... 105

Nurturing Your Faith Throughout the Journey 106

"Rebuilding and Growing: Navigating the Emotional Landscape" 107

Rebuilding Trust 108

Dealing with Emotional Numbness 109

Breaking Free from Feeling Stuck 110

Cultivating Patience and Self-Compassion 111

Chapter 13: "Embracing Your Voice: Final Thoughts and Encouragement" 113

Recap of the Journey 113

The Ongoing Nature of Growth 114

Embracing Your Authentic Self 114

The Ripple Effect of Healthy Communication 115

A Message of Hope 115

Final Call to Action 116

Closing Thoughts 116

Resources 118

INTRODUCTION: BREAKING THE SILENCE

Have you ever felt like you're talking to a wall? Like your partner has suddenly become a ghost in your own home? If so, you've probably experienced the silent treatment, and let me tell you, you're not alone.

I'm Cheryl, and I've been there. For years, I walked on eggshells in my relationships, constantly wondering what I'd done wrong when my partner would suddenly shut down and shut me out. The silence was deafening, and the confusion and hurt were overwhelming. It's a journey that many of us have walked, often feeling isolated and unsure of where to turn.

But here's what I want you to know from the start: You didn't do anything wrong. The silent treatment isn't about you - it's about control. It's a tool that narcissists and emotional abusers use to manipulate and hurt their partners. And it's not okay.

Understanding the Silent Treatment

The silent treatment is more than just a communication breakdown. It's a form of emotional abuse that can have profound effects on your mental health, self-esteem, and overall well-being. It's a way for the abuser to exert power, punish, and control their partner without having to engage in direct conflict.

Many of us who have experienced this form of abuse find ourselves questioning our own sanity. We replay conversations in our heads, wondering what we said or did to deserve such treatment. We might even start to believe that if we were just "better" - more attentive, more understanding, more perfect - the silence would end.

But the truth is, the silent treatment says more about the person using it than it does about the person on the receiving end. It's a sign of emotional immaturity and an inability to communicate in healthy, respectful ways.

The Impact of Silent Treatment

The effects of silent treatment can be devastating and long-lasting. It can lead to anxiety, depression, and a deep sense of unworthiness. It can make you question your perception of reality and damage your ability to trust, not just in your current relationship, but in future ones as well.

I remember feeling like I was constantly walking on eggshells, afraid that any misstep would cause days or weeks of icy silence. The stress took a toll on my physical health, my work performance, and my relationships with friends and family. Maybe you've experienced similar effects in your own life.

The Purpose of This Book

In this book, I will share everything I've learned about dealing with the silent treatment—not as a doctor or a therapist, but as someone who's lived it, breathed it, and found ways to break free from its suffocating grip. We'll explore the psychology behind this form of abuse, its various manifestations, and most importantly, practical strategies for reclaiming your voice and your power.

We will discuss:

- Why people use the silent treatment
- How it affects you emotionally, mentally, and physically
- Strategies for coping with and responding to silent treatment
- How to set boundaries and protect your mental health
- Ways to rebuild your self-esteem and confidence
- Techniques for improving communication in your relationships
- When and how to seek professional help
- How to recognize when it's time to leave an abusive relationship
- Steps for healing and moving forward, whether you stay or go
- And many more

This book is about more than just understanding silent treatment. It's about reclaiming your worth, your voice, and your right to be heard. It's about learning to demand the respect and open communication you deserve in all your relationships.

A Personal Journey

As we embark on this journey together, I want you to know that I understand the pain, confusion, and self-doubt you might be feeling. I've been there. I've felt the sting of being ignored, the frustration of trying to communicate with someone who refuses to engage, and the deep loneliness that comes from feeling invisible in your own relationship.

But I also want you to know there is hope. With understanding, support, and the right tools, it is possible to break free from the cycle of silent treatment. Whether that means healing your current relationship or finding the strength to leave, you have the power to create a life filled with healthy, respectful communication.

This book is the result of years of personal experience, research, and conversations with others who have faced similar struggles. It's the book I wish I had when I was in the thick of it, feeling lost and alone.

As you read, remember you are not alone. Your feelings are valid, your experiences matter, and you deserve to be treated with respect and kindness. Let this book be your guide, your support, and your reminder that you are worthy of love, respect, and open, honest communication.

So if you're ready to stop the silence and start living on your terms, let's dive in. Your journey to reclaiming your voice starts now.

CHAPTER I

"THE SILENT TREATMENT: A NARCISSIST'S ABUSIVE PARTNER'S SECRET WEAPON"

Understanding the Power Dynamic

Friends, I've learned the hard way: the silent treatment isn't just annoying - it's toxic. It's like a slow-acting poison in your relationship, and it's one of the favorite tricks in a narcissist's or abusive partner's playbook. To truly grasp why it's so harmful, we need to delve into the power dynamics at play.

At its core, the silent treatment is about control and dominance. It's a form of emotional manipulation that creates an imbalance of power in the relationship. The person using silent treatment holds all the cards - they decide when communication starts and stops, effectively controlling the emotional temperature of the relationship.

When my partner first started giving me the silent treatment, I was confused. Was he just cooling off? Did he need space? These are normal, healthy behaviors in a relationship, right? But as time passed, I realized this was about something far more treacherous than needing space. It was about power.

Here's the deal: Narcissists and abusive partners use the silent treatment as a calculated tactic. They're not ignoring you because they're hurt or need time to think. They're doing it because they know it drives you crazy. They understand that humans are social creatures who crave connection and validation. By withholding these basic needs, they create a sense of emotional deprivation that can be unbearable.

This tactic is particularly effective because it plays on our deepest insecurities and fears. When someone we love suddenly withdraws, it triggers primal fears of abandonment. We start to question ourselves: "What did I do wrong? Am I not good enough? How can I fix this?" This self-doubt is exactly what the abuser wants.

I remember spending days, even weeks, trying to figure out what I'd done wrong. I'd rack my brain, analyzing every conversation, every interaction. I found myself apologizing for things I hadn't even done, just to get a word out of my partner. And that's precisely what they want - to see you scramble, to watch you twist yourself into knots trying to please them.

But I want you to understand something crucial: this isn't about you. It's about them. The silent treatment is a way for narcissists and abusive partners to:

1. *Punish you for not meeting their unrealistic expectations:* By withdrawing affection and communication, they're essentially putting you in an emotional "time-out" like a child. This infantilizes you and reinforces their position of authority in the relationship.
2. *Make you feel small and insignificant:* When someone acts as if you don't exist, it chips away at your sense of self-worth. Over time, this can lead to a diminished sense of self and increased dependence on the abuser for validation.
3. *Avoid taking responsibility for their actions:* Silent treatment allows the abuser to sidestep difficult conversations or accountability. Instead of addressing issues directly, they create a situation where you're so desperate for their attention that you'll let their bad behavior slide.
4. *Keep you walking on eggshells, always trying to please them:* The unpredictability of silent treatment creates a state of constant anxiety. You never know what might trigger another bout of silence, so you become hypervigilant, always trying to keep your partner happy to avoid the "punishment" of being ignored.
5. *Maintain control over the relationship:* By dictating when and how communication happens, the abuser holds all the power. They get to decide

when the silence ends, often acting as if nothing happened, which further disorients and confuses you.

6. ***Create emotional dependency:*** Paradoxically, the silent treatment can make you more emotionally dependent on your abuser. The relief you feel when they finally acknowledge you again can create a trauma bond, making it harder to leave the relationship.

Understanding these dynamics is crucial because it helps you see the silent treatment for what it truly is - a form of emotional abuse. It's not a normal communication style or a quirk to be tolerated. It's a deliberate strategy designed to manipulate and control you.

Recognizing this can be a pivotal moment in your journey. It shifts the narrative from "What's wrong with me?" to "What's wrong with this behavior?" This understanding is the first step towards regaining your power and changing the dynamics of your relationship.

The Psychology Behind Silent Treatment

It's manipulation, pure and simple. And recognizing it for what it is? That's your first step towards breaking free from its power. But to truly understand and combat this behavior, we need to delve deeper into the psychology behind it.

At its core, the silent treatment is a form of social rejection - a tactic that humans have used for thousands of years to punish and control others. Social psychology research has shown that being ignored or excluded activates the same brain regions as physical pain. This explains why the silent treatment can feel so devastating - your brain literally processes it as a form of injury.

Dr. Kipling Williams, psychology professor at Purdue University, has extensively studied social exclusion. He found that being ignored threatens four fundamental human needs:

1. Belonging: The need to feel connected to others.
2. Self-esteem: The need to feel good about ourselves.
3. Control: The need to feel we have some influence over our lives.
4. Meaningful existence: The need to feel our lives have purpose and we matter to others.

The silent treatment effectively attacks all of these needs simultaneously, which is why it's such a powerful and damaging tactic.

From the perspective of the person using silent treatment, it's often a learned behavior. They may have grown up in an environment where this was a common tactic, or they may have discovered its effectiveness through trial and error. For individuals with narcissistic tendencies or other personality disorders, it can be a go-to method for maintaining control and avoiding accountability.

Let me share a personal story that drove this home for me. Once, I forgot to pick up my partner's dry cleaning because I was swamped at work. Instead of expressing disappointment or even anger, he vanished—emotionally. He was physically present but wouldn't speak to me, look at me, or acknowledge my existence for three days.

I was devastated. I apologized profusely, promised to do better, and even offered to do all the errands for a month. But nothing broke the silence. It wasn't until I stopped reacting and begging for forgiveness that he suddenly 'forgave' me and started talking again.

This experience illustrates several psychological principles at work:

1. ***Behavior Conditioning:*** By withholding attention (a form of punishment) and then suddenly providing it (reinforcement), my partner was essentially training me to behave in ways he desired.
2. ***Unpredictable Reinforcement:*** The uncertainty of when the silence would end creates a powerful psychological hook, similar to the mechanism that makes gambling addictive.
3. ***Cognitive Dissonance:*** The contrast between the severity of the 'punishment' and the minor nature of my mistake created psychological discomfort, leading me to inflate the importance of the dry cleaning to justify the reaction.
4. ***Trauma Bonding:*** The relief I felt when he finally spoke to me again created an unhealthy attachment, strengthening the cycle of abuse.

That's when I realized this wasn't about dry cleaning. It was about making me so desperate for his approval that I'd do anything to get it.

The silent treatment can take many forms:

1. Completely ignoring you
2. Giving one-word answers
3. Refusing to make eye contact
4. Shutting down all physical affection
5. Acting like you're invisible in social situations

Each of these forms plays on our deep-seated need for connection and validation. They create a sense of emotional starvation that can be unbearable.

From a psychological standpoint, the silent treatment is particularly cunning because it's a passive-aggressive tactic. Unlike open aggression, which is easy to identify and call out, the silent treatment allows the abuser to claim innocence. "I'm not doing anything," they might say if confronted. This gaslighting aspect adds another layer of psychological harm, making the victim question their own perceptions and reactions.

"Moreover, silent treatment takes advantage of our brain's natural tendency to focus more on bad experiences than good ones. This is sometimes called our 'focus on the bad.' It's a trait that helped our ancestors stay safe by being alert to dangers. In relationships, this means that the painful periods of silent treatment can overshadow and outweigh the good times, slowly damaging the overall quality of the relationship."

But here's the truth I want you to hold onto: You're not powerless or alone, and you deserve better than the silent treatment. Understanding the psychology behind this behavior is crucial because it shifts the focus from self-blame to recognizing it as a harmful tactic.

"Understanding why abusers use silent treatment is crucial, but it's equally important to recognize its various forms. In the next chapter, we'll explore the different faces of silence and how they manifest in relationships."

CHAPTER 2

"THE MANY FACES OF SILENCE: TYPES OF SILENT TREATMENT"

When I first started dealing with the silent treatment, I thought it was always the same - just flat-out ignoring. But as I've lived through it and talked with other women, I've realized that the silent treatment can wear many masks. Let me break it down for you:

The Complete Shutdown

The classic silent treatment. Your partner acts like you've suddenly become invisible. They won't speak to you, look at you, or acknowledge your presence. It's like you've ceased to exist in their world.

I remember one Christmas when my partner was upset about something (to this day, I'm not sure what). He sat through our entire family dinner without saying a word to me. My relatives kept giving me confused looks, and I felt like I was going crazy. That's the power of this type of silence - it makes you question your reality.

The Complete Shutdown can last hours, days or even weeks. During this time, your partner might:

- Walk past you in the house without acknowledging you
- Ignore your questions or comments completely
- Leave the room when you enter
- Refuse to eat meals with you
- Sleep in a separate room without explanation

The psychological impact of this can be severe. You might find yourself desperately trying to 'fix' whatever you think you've done wrong, even when you don't know what it is. The silent treatment is what your narcissistic/abusive partner wants. It's a tactic to keep you off-balance and anxious.

The Minimal Responder

This is a sneakier form of silent treatment. Your partner will respond to you, but only with grunts, one-word answers, or the bare minimum communication necessary. They're technically talking, but there's no real engagement.

"How was your day?" I'd ask. "Fine," he mutters without looking up from his phone. "Do you want to go out for dinner?" "Whatever."

It's maddening because they can always claim they're not ignoring you. But trust me, this is just as manipulative as the complete shutdown.

The Minimal Responder might:

- Use non-committal sounds like "Mhm" or "Uh-huh" instead of actual words
- Give short, uninformative answers that don't invite further conversation
- Respond to texts with single words or emojis, even to essential questions
- Avoid eye contact while giving these minimal responses
- Use a flat or disinterested tone of voice

This type of silent treatment is insidious because it can make you feel you overreact. After all, they're responding. However, the lack of real engagement is a form of emotional withdrawal that can be just as painful as complete silence.

The Selective Silence

This silence is when your partner usually talks to everyone else but gives you the cold shoulder. They'll chat happily with friends, family, even strangers, but suddenly, they have nothing to say when it comes to you.

I once hosted a dinner party where my partner was the life of the party—laughing, joking, and telling stories. But whenever I spoke to him directly, he'd suddenly become mute or give me a one-word response. It was humiliating and confusing for me, and it sent a clear message to our guests that something was 'wrong' with me.

The Selective Silent Treatment might involve:

- Ignoring you in group settings while engaging enthusiastically with others
- Talking over you or cutting you out of conversations
- Responding warmly to others' messages or calls but ignoring yours
- Being chatty and upbeat with others immediately before or after giving you the cold shoulder
- Using others to communicate with you instead of speaking to you directly

This form of silent treatment is particularly hurtful because it isolates you socially and can damage your other relationships. It's designed to make you look and feel like the problem.

The Ghosting Silent Treatment

This one's becoming more common in the age of technology. Your partner disappears—no calls, texts, or social media responses. They're physically absent and unreachable.

During one awful period, my partner disappeared for three days. No warning, no explanation. I was sick with worry, imagining all sorts of horrible scenarios. When he finally reappeared, he acted like nothing had happened. That's when I realized this disappearing act was another form of control.

Ghosting might involve:

- Suddenly becoming unreachable by phone, text, or social media
- Disappearing for hours or days without explanation
- Failing to show up for planned events or dates without notice
- Being active on social media but ignoring your messages
- Reappearing as if nothing happened, often without apology or explanation

Ghosting can be especially anxiety-inducing because it plays on fears of abandonment and can leave you in a state of constant uncertainty.

The Passive-Aggressive Communicator

This person will communicate in a way designed to make you feel guilty or small. They'll sigh heavily, roll their eyes, or use a tone that says, "I'm only talking to you because I have to."

"I guess I'll do the dishes AGAIN," they might say, implying you never help out (even if you do).

Passive-aggressive silent treatment might include:

- Making pointed comments about your behavior without directly addressing issues
- Using sarcasm or a condescending tone when speaking to you
- Giving backhanded compliments
- Making plans without including you, then acting surprised that you feel left out
- Agreeing to do things but then 'forgetting' or doing them poorly

This form of silent treatment is particularly confusing because there is communication, but it's negative and indirect. It can leave you feeling guilty, defensive, and unsure of where you stand.

Recognizing these different types of silent treatment is crucial because it helps you see manipulation for what it is. It's not just 'how they are' or 'how they deal with conflict.' It's a calculated method of controlling you and your emotions.

In the next chapter, we'll discuss how to respond to these types of silent treatment. But for now, I want you to know that if you've experienced any of these, you're not alone. More importantly, you don't deserve it.

Either way, silent treatment is a form of emotional abuse. You deserve open, honest communication in your relationships. Don't let anyone make you believe otherwise."

"Now that we can identify different types of silent treatment, it's time to examine how this behavior affects you. The next chapter will dive into the emotional, psychological, and physical impacts of enduring silent treatment."

CHAPTER 3

"THE SILENT WOUNDS: HOW THE SILENT TREATMENT AFFECTS YOU"

When I first started experiencing the silent treatment, I thought I was just being 'too sensitive.' But over time, I realized that this silent abuse was leaving very real scars on my heart and mind. Let me share with you what I've learned about the devastating effects of the silent treatment.

It Destroys Your Self-Esteem

Remember how I told you about that Christmas dinner where my partner wouldn't speak to me? By the end of that night, I was convinced I was the scariest person in the world. I kept thinking, 'I must be truly awful if he can't even bring himself to speak to me.'

That's what the silent treatment does. It makes you question your worth. You start to think:

- 'Maybe I don't deserve to be spoken to.'

- 'I must be a horrible person to be treated this way.'
- 'If only I were better/smarter/prettier, they wouldn't ignore me.'

Let me be clear: These thoughts are NOT true. They're the result of the emotional manipulation you're experiencing.

Self-esteem destruction doesn't happen overnight. It's a slow erosion like waves constantly battering a shoreline. Each instance of silent treatment chips away at your sense of self-worth. You might find yourself:

- Apologizing constantly, even for things that aren't your fault
- Changing your behavior, appearance, or opinions to try to please your partner
- Feeling unworthy of love or affection
- Believing that you're lucky they're with you despite the abuse

I remember looking in the mirror one day and not recognizing the woman staring back at me. I had lost weight from the stress, my eyes were constantly puffy from crying, and I had stopped wearing the bright colors I used to love because they 'annoyed' my partner. That's when I realized how much of myself I had lost trying to be 'good enough' to deserve basic communication.

It Creates Anxiety and Depression

The silent treatment left me in a constant state of anxiety. I was always on edge, wondering when the next bout of silence would come. Would it be because I didn't load the dishwasher right? Because I laughed too loud at a joke?

This constant state of worry can lead to full-blown anxiety and depression. You might experience:

- Trouble sleeping or eating
- Difficulty concentrating at work
- Constant feelings of dread or sadness
- Physical symptoms like headaches or stomach aches

Anxiety doesn't just appear during periods of silence. It becomes a constant companion. You're always waiting for the other shoe to drop, trying to gauge your partner's mood and predict when the next silent treatment might occur.

I developed insomnia during my relationship. Every night, I'd lie awake, replaying every interaction from the day, trying to figure out if I'd done something to trigger my partner's silence. Knowing the peace was likely temporary, I couldn't relax even on good days.

Depression often follows. The constant emotional roller coaster is exhausting. You might find yourself:

- Losing interest in activities you once enjoyed
- Isolating yourself from friends and family

- Feeling hopeless about the future
- Having thoughts of self-harm or suicide

If you're experiencing these symptoms, please seek professional help. You don't have to face this alone.

It Makes You Doubt Your Perception of Reality

Sometimes, after days of silence, my partner would act like nothing had happened. He'd suddenly be chatty and affectionate, leaving me wondering if I'd imagined the whole thing.

This is called gaslighting, a common tactic used alongside the silent treatment. It makes you question your memories and perceptions, leaving you confused and off-balance.

The effects of this reality-twisting can be profound:

- You might start doubting your memory of events
- You could begin to question your judgment in other areas of life
- You may feel 'going crazy' or 'too sensitive.'
- You might stop trusting your perceptions and rely on the abuser to define reality for you

I kept a journal to record what was happening because I couldn't trust my memory anymore. Looking back at those entries now, I'm shocked at how much I was willing to excuse or forget to maintain the relationship.

It Damages Your Other Relationships

The effects of silent treatment don't stop in your relationship with your partner. It can poison your other relationships, too. You might:

- Become withdrawn from friends and family, fearing you'll be ignored by them too
- Overreact to perceived slights from others, continually fearing rejection
- Have trouble trusting people or opening up emotionally

I've lost touch with so many friends during my relationship. At first, it was because I was embarrassed about what was happening at home. Later, it was because I had forgotten how to have healthy interactions with people every day.

Even now, I cringe when friends don't respond to texts immediately, convinced they're also giving me the silent treatment. It takes time to rebuild your trust in others and yourself, even as you're working on your primary relationship.

The silent treatment creates a ripple effect that impacts all your connections. You might find yourself:

- Hesitating to make plans with friends, worried you'll have to cancel if your partner decides to 'go silent.'

- Avoiding confiding in family members about your relationship struggles
- Becoming overly anxious about any perceived distance in friendships
- Struggling to maintain professional relationships due to decreased self-confidence

I remember when a close friend didn't reply to my message for a day. I was anxious, convinced she was mad at me or giving me the silent treatment. It took me a while to realize that this reaction resulted from the dynamic in my relationship, not a reflection of my friendship.

Working on these external relationships while navigating the challenges in your primary relationship is difficult, but it's crucial for your overall well-being. Having a support system outside your relationship can provide perspective and emotional support as you work through these issues."

It Can Lead to Physical Health Problems

The stress of constant emotional abuse can affect your physical health. Research has shown that social rejection pain activates the same brain areas as physical pain. This chronic stress can lead to:

- Weakened immune system
- Cardiovascular problems
- Chronic pain
- Digestive issues

During the worst periods of silent treatment, I was constantly sick. I caught every cold going around, developed chronic migraines, and had persistent stomach issues. It wasn't until I left the relationship that I realized how much the emotional stress had been affecting my physical health.

The body keeps the score, as they say. Even if you're trying to ignore the emotional pain, your body will find ways to tell you that something is wrong.

It Makes You Lose Your Voice

One of the most insidious effects of the silent treatment is how it silences you. You become so afraid of triggering another silence that you start censoring yourself. You stop expressing your needs, your opinions, your very self.

I remember when I was bursting to share some good news about a promotion at work. But my partner had been giving me the cold shoulder all week, and I was terrified of saying the wrong thing. So I stayed quiet, swallowing my joy and excitement. That's when I realized how much of myself I'd lost to this abuse.

This self-silencing can manifest in many ways:

- You might stop sharing your opinions on anything from politics to what movie to watch
- You could find yourself unable to ask for what you need, even in other relationships
- You might lose touch with your own desires and goals, focusing only on avoiding conflict

- You could develop a fear of speaking up in any situation, even at work or with friends

I used to be known for my loud, unrestrained, joyful laugh. But after years of being told I was 'too loud' and receiving the silent treatment for expressing myself, I found I had almost forgotten how to laugh. Reclaiming my voice, literally and figuratively, was one of the most challenging but rewarding parts of my healing journey.

Remember this: Your voice matters. Your thoughts, feelings, and experiences are valid and deserving of expression.

The silent treatment is not just 'silent.' It speaks volumes about the abuser's lack of respect and empathy for you. It's a form of emotional violence that leaves real, lasting damage.

But here's the good news: recognizing these effects is the first step towards healing. In the next chapter, we'll talk about how to start reclaiming your voice and your power. Because you deserve to be heard, always."

Remember, every relationship is unique, and there's no one-size-fits-all solution. But you can work towards a healthier, more communicative relationship by understanding the effects of silent treatment and learning how to address it."

"Understanding the effects of silent treatment is the first step towards healing. In the following chapter, we'll explore practical strategies for breaking the silence and addressing this harmful behavior in your relationship."

CHAPTER 4

"BREAKING THE SILENCE: STRATEGIES FOR DEALING WITH SILENT TREATMENT"

Living with silent treatment isn't easy, but there are ways to cope and even work towards positive change. Here are some strategies I've learned and am still practicing in my relationship:

Recognize It's Not Your Fault

Primarily, understand that you're not responsible for your partner's behavior. The silent treatment is a choice they're making, and it's not because you're unworthy of communication.

I used to rack my brain to figure out what I'd done wrong. I remind myself, "His silence is about him, not me."

If this is difficult: Try writing down your feelings. Often, seeing our thoughts on paper helps us recognize when we're being too hard on ourselves. Create a list of positive qualities and read it when self-doubt creeps in.

If staying: Build your self-esteem independent of your partner's behavior. Consider therapy to help reinforce this.

If leaving: Use this realization as a stepping stone to recognize other ways you might have incorrectly blamed yourself in the relationship.

Don't Chase the Silent Partner

It's tempting to try to force communication - to beg, plead, or demand answers. But this often plays into the silent partner's hands, giving them the desired reaction.

Instead, I've learned to permit myself to step back. I'll say, "You're not ready to talk right now. I'll be here when you are." Then, I focus on my activities.

You should be more direct if this doesn't work or the silence persists. Try saying, "I understand you need space, but complete silence for days harms our relationship. Can we agree on a time to talk about this?"

If you're staying: Consistently apply this approach. It may take time, but it can help break the cycle of silent treatment.

If you're leaving: This skill of not chasing approval will serve you well in future relationships and in building your independence.

Set Clear Boundaries

It's important to communicate that silent treatment isn't acceptable. When your partner communicates again, calmly discuss how their behavior affects you.

I've said, "When you give me the silent treatment, I feel hurt and disrespected. If you need space in the future, please tell me that directly?"

If boundaries aren't respected, consistently reinforce them. Each time the silent treatment occurs, calmly remind your partner of the agreement you made.

If you're staying: Be prepared to enforce consequences if boundaries are repeatedly violated. This might mean taking some time apart or seeking couples therapy.

If you're leaving: Use this experience to help you establish clear boundaries early in future relationships.

Practice Self-Care

During periods of silence, focus on taking care of yourself. You're not being selfish - it's necessary.

Make sure to eat well, exercise, and do things you enjoy. Sometimes, I'll call a friend or family member for a chat. Taking care of myself helps me stay grounded.

If you're struggling with self-care, Start small. Set a simple daily self-care goal, like taking a 10-minute walk or reading a chapter of a book you enjoy.

If you're staying, Make self-care a non-negotiable part of your routine, regardless of what's happening in your relationship.

If you're leaving, Continue prioritizing self-care as you navigate the challenges of ending the relationship and moving forward.

Keep Communication Open on Your End

While respecting their need for space, let your partner know you're open to talking when they're ready. This can be as simple as a daily "I'm here when you want to talk."

If this needs to be fixed, try varying your approach. Instead of words, leave a note or suggest a nonverbal way of indicating they're ready to talk, like squeezing your hand.

If you're staying: Maintain this open line of communication, but be careful not to let it turn into pleading or chasing.

If you're leaving: Recognize your willingness to communicate openly, a strength you'll carry into future relationships.

Seek Professional Help

If silent treatment is a persistent issue, consider couples therapy. A professional can provide tools for better communication and help address underlying issues.

It took some convincing, but my partner and I started seeing a therapist. It's been challenging, but we're learning healthier ways to communicate.

If your partner refuses therapy, Don't let this stop you from seeking help yourself. Individual therapy can provide valuable support and tools for managing the situation.

If you're staying, Use therapy to improve your relationship dynamics continually.

If you're leaving, Individual therapy can provide crucial support as you navigate ending the relationship and healing.

Know Your Limits

While working on the relationship is admirable, knowing your limits is vital. Continuous silent treatment is a form of emotional abuse.

I've had to seriously consider what I'm willing to accept in my relationship. It's an ongoing process, but I'm committed to maintaining my self-respect and emotional well-being.

If you're struggling to enforce limits, Seek support from trusted friends, family, or a therapist. An outside perspective can help you see when a situation has become unhealthy.

If you are staying, regularly reassess your limits. Are they being respected? Has the situation improved? Be honest with yourself about the answers.

If you're leaving, Use your understanding of your limits to guide you in future relationships. Your ability to recognize and enforce your boundaries is a valuable skill.

Remember, your well-being should be your top priority whether you stay or leave. If you stay, it's because you see genuine effort and improvement, not because you're afraid to go. If you leave, you realize you deserve a relationship without emotional manipulation.

If you're staying: Commit to ongoing work on the relationship. Celebrate improvements, but remain vigilant about your boundaries and needs.

If you're leaving, Be proud of your strength. Seek support, take care of yourself, and know you're making this decision out of self-respect and self-love.

In either case, remember that you deserve open, honest, and respectful communication in all your relationships. The work you're doing now—improving your relationship or preparing to leave—is invaluable for your future happiness and well-being."

"Armed with strategies to address silent treatment, it's important to prepare for the journey ahead. The next chapter will focus on maintaining your progress and handling inevitable setbacks along the way."

CHAPTER 5

"STAYING STRONG: MAINTAINING PROGRESS AND HANDLING SETBACKS"

Dealing with silent treatment is not a one-time fix. It's an ongoing process that requires patience, persistence, and self-compassion. Here's what I've learned about maintaining progress and handling the inevitable setbacks:

Celebrate Small Victories

When you're in the thick of it, focusing only on the problems is easy. However, recognizing and celebrating minor improvements is crucial for maintaining hope and motivation.

In my relationship, I started noting every instance where we communicated effectively during a disagreement. It might have been as simple as my partner saying, "I need some time," instead of going silent or expressing my feelings without getting defensive.

These small wins might seem insignificant, but they're the building blocks of change. Acknowledge, celebrate, and use them as motivation to keep going.

If this doesn't work, If you're struggling to see any victories, no matter how small, it might be time to redefine what progress looks like. Maybe it's about something other than your partner's behavior changing but your responses improving. Celebrate your growth and resilience.

If you're staying, Continue to acknowledge even the tiniest improvements. Use these as conversation starters with your partner about what's working.

If you're leaving, Recognize that your ability to spot positive changes is a valuable skill you'll carry into future relationships. It also shows your capacity for hope and optimism, which will serve you well as you progress.

Expect and Prepare for Setbacks

Progress isn't linear. There will be times when it feels like you're back at square one. It doesn't mean you have failed.

I remember feeling devastated the first time my partner resorted to silent treatment after weeks of improvement. But I've learned that setbacks are a normal part of the process.

Prepare for these moments:

- Have a self-care plan ready for when setbacks occur
- Remind yourself of the progress you've made so far
- Reach out to your support system when you're feeling discouraged

If setbacks are constant: If you're experiencing more setbacks than progress, it might be time to reassess your approach. Consider seeking professional help to develop new strategies.

If you are staying, Use setbacks as opportunities for open discussion with your partner. Try to identify triggers and work together on prevention strategies.

If you are leaving, Recognize that your ability to handle setbacks is a strength. This resilience will be valuable as you navigate the challenges of ending the relationship and moving on.

Keep Learning and Growing

Continual personal growth is critical to maintaining progress. This isn't about changing yourself to prevent silent treatment – it's about becoming stronger and more resilient.

I've found immense value in reading books on communication, attending personal development workshops, and continuing with individual therapy. The more I understand myself and healthy relationship dynamics, the better equipped I am to navigate challenges.

If growth feels stagnant: If you feel stuck, try exploring a new area of personal development. It may be time to focus on self-compassion or learn to set healthy boundaries.

If you are staying, Invite your partner to join you in learning. Sharing resources and discussing your learning can bring you closer and foster mutual growth.

If you are leaving, your commitment to personal growth will serve you well as you move forward. Continue investing in yourself—this is the foundation for healthier future relationships.

Regularly Reassess Your Boundaries

As you grow and your relationship evolves, your boundaries need adjusting. What you were willing to accept early in the process might no longer align with your needs.

Every few months, I take time to reflect on my boundaries. Are they being respected? Do they still serve me? Should they be strengthened or clarified?

If your partner continually disrespects your boundaries, enforcing consequences is crucial. This might mean taking space, seeking counseling, or reconsidering the relationship.

If you're staying, Communicate your boundaries and the consequences for violating them. Be prepared to follow through consistently.

If you're leaving: *\,* Use this experience to inform the boundaries you'll set in future relationships. Recognize that your growing ability to establish and maintain boundaries is a valuable skill.

Maintain Your Identity Outside the Relationship

It's easy to become so focused on improving your relationship that you lose sight of who you are as an individual. However, maintaining your identity is crucial for your well-being and relationship health.

I nurture my interests, friendships, and goals. This makes me happier and brings fresh energy into my relationships.

If you've lost yourself, Start small. Reconnect with an old hobby, reach out to a friend, or set a personal goal unrelated to your relationship.

If you are staying, Encourage your partner to do the same. A relationship is healthiest when both people have full, independent lives outside it.

If you are leaving, your established independent identity will be crucial support as you transition out of the relationship. Keep investing in your interests and relationships.

Practice Ongoing Communication

Don't wait for problems to arise to talk about communication. Make it a regular practice to check in with each other about how you're feeling and what you need.

My partner and I have started having weekly 'relationship check-ins.' We discuss what's gone well, our challenges, and how we can support each other in the coming week.

If communication remains difficult, Consider using structured communication tools, like "I feel" statements or the Gottman Institute's State of the Union meeting format.

If you are staying, Consistently make time for these check-ins, even when things are going well. Regular communication can prevent issues from building up.

If you are leaving: The communication skills you've developed will be valuable in all your future relationships, romantic or otherwise.

Be Patient with Yourself and Your Partner

Lasting change takes time. Sometimes, you slip into old patterns or react in ways you're trying to change. Be patient and kind to yourself and your partner during these times.

I've learned to view these moments as opportunities for growth rather than failures. Each time we navigate a difficult situation, we learn more about ourselves and each other.

If patience is wearing thin, acknowledge your frustration. Take some time to reset. Remember that your patience can be limited.

If you're staying, *Communicate your* frustration to your partner. Work together to set realistic expectations for change.

If you're leaving: Recognize that your patience and effort demonstrate your capacity for commitment. These are valuable qualities that you'll carry into future relationships.

Remember, your work on yourself is invaluable whether you choose to stay or leave. If you stay, it contributes to a healthier relationship. If you go, it prepares you for healthier future relationships and a stronger sense of self.

The decision to stay or leave is deeply personal and depends on many factors. Are you seeing genuine effort and change from your partner? Do you feel respected and valued most of the time? Are your core needs being met? Only you can answer these questions.

If you choose to stay, commit to improving communication and maintaining your boundaries. If you decide to leave, be proud of your strength to make that decision. Seek support, take care of yourself, and know that you deserve a relationship free from emotional manipulation.

In either case, remember that you deserve respect, love, and open, honest communication. Your feelings are valid, your needs matter, and you have the right to be treated with kindness and consideration."

"As you continue to make progress, it's time to focus on deeper, long-term healing. In the next chapter, we'll explore strategies for personal growth and overcoming the lasting effects of silent treatment."

CHAPTER 6

"HEALING AND GROWING: LONG-TERM STRATEGIES FOR OVERCOMING SILENT TREATMENT"

Rebuild Your Self-Esteem

Silent treatment is like acid rain on your self-esteem, slowly eroding your sense of worth. Rebuilding it isn't just important – it's essential for survival and growth.

I remember staring at a blank page one day, feeling as empty as the paper before me. That's when I knew I had to change. I started small with a simple 'self-esteem jar.' Every night, I'd write down one thing I was proud of that day – no matter how tiny – and put it in the jar. On my lowest days, I'd pull out those slips of paper and read them, reminding myself of my strengths and accomplishments.

As I grew stronger, I expanded this practice. I started taking myself on 'self-love dates'—solo trips to art supply stores, fancy stationery shops, and a weekend writing retreat. It felt awkward initially, but I soon looked forward to it.

"For me, remembering that I am created with inherent worth and purpose has been a powerful antidote to the self-doubt caused by silent treatment. This belief anchors me when other sources of validation are silent.

If this feels overwhelming, Start with a 'gratitude minute.' Set a timer for 60 seconds each morning and list out loud everything you're grateful for about yourself. It might feel forced at first, but stick with it. You're retraining your brain to focus on your positive qualities.

If you're staying, Invite your partner to join you in appreciation exercises. Each day, share one thing you appreciate about each other. This not only boosts your self-esteem but can also help shift the relationship dynamic.

If you're leaving, Use your renewed sense of self-worth as a compass. Make decisions based on what the confident, self-assured you would want, not you that's been diminished by the silent treatment.

Develop Emotional Intelligence

Understanding your emotions is like learning a new language – the language of your inner self. When you're fluent in this language, you're better equipped to handle the silent treatment and all of life's challenges.

For me, the breakthrough came with an unexpected source: emotion mapping. Throughout the day, I'd pause and ask myself, "What am I feeling right now?" I'd identify the emotion as precisely as possible and locate where I felt it in my body. Anxiety might be a tightness in my chest, while excitement about a new book idea could be a flutter in my stomach.

I jotted these observations down in a small notebook I carried. Over time, this practice helped me recognize my emotional patterns. I often felt a knot in my stomach right before my partner withdrew into silence. Recognizing this allowed me to address issues proactively, sometimes preventing the silent treatment altogether.

This approach helped me respond to silent treatment with more clarity and less reactivity. Instead of spiraling into anxiety or self-doubt, I could observe my emotions and choose my response.

If traditional methods aren't working, Incorporate your emotions into your creative work. For me I found writing a poem about how silence feels, and creating handmade books helped in my emotional journey.

If you are staying, Share your emotional discoveries with your partner. You might say, "I've noticed I tend to feel anxiety in my chest when communication breaks down. Can we work together on staying connected, even during disagreements?"

If you are leaving, your enhanced emotional intelligence will be your superpower in future relationships. You'll be able to articulate your needs clearly and understand others' emotions more intensely.

Build a Strong Support Network

Amid silent treatment, it's easy to feel like you're on a deserted island. Building a support network is like creating a fleet of rescue boats – always ready when needed.

I had to rebuild my support network from scratch. Years of silent treatment had left me isolated. I started with a writing group—low-pressure, with a built-in conversation topic. One of my writers is now one of my closest friends. We have a standing weekly coffee date where we discuss our latest projects and life challenges.

I also tried 'friendship dating.' I set a goal to reach out to one new person each week—another local author, a fellow bookbinder, or even someone whose balloon art I admired on Instagram. I'd start with a simple interaction, maybe commenting on their work or asking about a shared interest. If it went well, I'd suggest a 'friendship date' – a coffee meet-up, a video call, or even collaborating on a small project.

Through this method, I connected with another local author. Our coffee 'date' became a regular writing accountability partnership, providing emotional support and professional growth.

If social anxiety is holding you back, Join online communities related to your interests. For example, join forums or social media groups for writers, bookbinders, or balloon artists. Shared interest provides an easy conversation starter.

If you're staying, Maintain these connections even as your relationship improves. Encourage your partner to build their support network, too. Healthy relationships thrive when both people have solid outside connections.

Your support network will be crucial during the transition if you're leaving. Don't be afraid to lean on them. Remember, seeking help is a sign of strength, not weakness.

Explore Your Passions

Rediscovering your passions is like finding a long-lost treasure map – it leads you back to the real you, the you that exists outside the relationship dynamics.

For me, it was my writing, bookbinding, and balloon art. I remember sitting at my desk, staring at a blank page, feeling as empty as the paper before me. The silent treatment had silenced my creativity, too. But I forced myself to write, even if it was nonsense initially. Gradually, words began to flow, and with them, my sense of self returned.

Crafting handmade books became a powerful metaphor for my healing journey. Each book was a fresh start, a new story waiting to be told. The act of binding pages together reminded me that I could bind the fragments of myself back into a whole.

Balloon art added an element of joy and playfulness to my healing. There's something magical about transforming a simple balloon into a work of art. It reminded me that I, too, could transform and take the heavy, painful experiences and reshape them into something beautiful.

I also tried 'passion sampling' to expand my world. I committed to trying a new activity every month – a pottery class one month, salsa dancing the next, and even theater. This approach led me to discover a love for improvisational theater, which has been incredibly healing. The principles of improv - accepting offers, building on ideas, embracing failure - have helped me navigate the unpredictability of my relationship and life.

If you're feeling stuck, Start with what you know. If you enjoy writing, try a new genre. If bookbinding is your thing, experiment with a new binding technique. The goal is to stretch yourself while still feeling grounded in what you love.

If you are staying, Use your rediscovered passions to bring new energy into your relationship. Share your enthusiasm with your partner, but also maintain boundaries. These passions are for you first.

If you are leaving, let your passions guide you in building your new life. They can lead to new friends, opportunities, and a renewed sense of purpose.

Learn About Healthy Relationships

Education is power, especially regarding understanding and cultivating healthy relationships. It's like getting a pair of glasses after years of blurry vision – you can see clearly what's healthy and what's not.

I devoured books on relationship psychology, but the real eye-opener came from an unexpected source: my creative pursuits. The process of writing taught me about the importance of pacing in relationships – knowing when to dive deep and when to give space. Bookbinding showed me the value of patience and precision in building something lasting. And balloon art? It reminded me that relationships, like balloons, need the right balance of give and take to maintain their shape without bursting.

This new understanding helped me recognize patterns in my relationship that I'd previously missed. It gave me a framework for discussing issues with my partner and set a new standard for what I wanted in our relationship.

If traditional learning methods don't appeal, Look for lessons in unexpected places. Observe the relationships around you – friends, family, and even characters in your favorite books. What dynamics do you admire? Which ones make you uncomfortable? Use these observations to shape your understanding of healthy relationships.

If you are staying, invite your partner to join you on this learning journey. You can take a relationship workshop together, read and discuss a book on healthy communication, or even collaborate on a creative project that explores relationship themes.

If you are leaving, Use this knowledge as a foundation for future relationships. You'll be in a stronger position to recognize red flags early and cultivate healthy dynamics from the start.

Remember, this journey of healing and growth is uniquely yours. Some days will be more challenging than others, and that's okay. Every word you write, every book you bind, every balloon you twist is an act of self-love and reclamation. You're not just creating art – you're recreating yourself. Whether you stay or leave, this work you're doing is invaluable. You're breaking cycles, setting new standards, and paving the way for a healthier, happier future. You've got this, and you're not alone."

As we continue our journey of healing, many find additional strength and comfort in their faith. In the next chapter, we'll explore how spiritual beliefs and practices can complement the strategies we've discussed and provide further support in overcoming the effects of silent treatment."

CHAPTER 7

"DRAWING STRENGTH FROM FAITH" CHAPTER:

In the journey of healing from silent treatment, many find solace and strength in their faith. Regardless of your specific beliefs, spirituality can provide a powerful foundation for recovery and personal growth. This chapter explores how faith can be a source of comfort, guidance, and resilience as you navigate the challenges of overcoming silent treatment.

It's important to note that faith is deeply personal. Whether you follow an organized religion, have a more individualized spiritual practice, or are just beginning to explore your beliefs, the principles discussed here can be adapted to fit your unique spiritual journey.

Finding Comfort in Spiritual Practices

When facing the pain of silent treatment, spiritual practices can offer a sanctuary of peace and comfort. Here are some ways to incorporate spiritual practices into your healing journey:

1. **Prayer and Meditation:** Set aside time each day for prayer or meditation. This can be as simple as a few minutes of quiet reflection or a more structured practice. Use this time to connect with your higher power, find inner calm, and seek guidance.
2. **Scripture Reading and Reflection**: If your faith includes sacred texts, spend time reading and reflecting on passages that speak to love, healing, and self-worth. Keep a journal to record your thoughts and insights.
3. **Attending Religious Services or Spiritual Gatherings**: Engaging with a community of like-minded individuals can provide support and a sense of belonging. If attending in person isn't possible, many faith communities offer online services or gatherings.
4. **Journaling with a Spiritual Focus:** Write about your spiritual experiences, questions, and growth. This can help you process your emotions and track your progress over time.

Using Faith as an Anchor in Difficult Times

When silent treatment leaves you feeling adrift, your faith can serve as a steady anchor. Here's how:

1. **Leaning on Faith-Based Support Systems**: Connect with religious leaders, spiritual mentors, or faith-based support groups. These individuals and communities can offer guidance, understanding, and encouragement.

2. **Finding Hope and Purpose Through Spiritual Teachings**: Many spiritual traditions offer teachings on overcoming adversity and finding meaning in suffering. Explore these teachings to gain perspective and hope.
3. **Practicing Forgiveness and Letting Go of Resentment:** While challenging, forgiveness can be a powerful tool for healing. Use your faith's teachings on forgiveness to guide you in releasing anger and resentment.
4. **Cultivating Gratitude and Focusing on Blessings:** Regularly acknowledge the good in your life, no matter how small. This practice can shift your focus from pain to positivity.

Integrating Faith into Your Healing Journey

Your faith can be woven into every aspect of your healing process:

1. **Aligning Healing Practices with Spiritual Beliefs:** As you work through the strategies discussed in previous chapters, consider how they align with your spiritual beliefs. For example, setting boundaries can be seen as an act of self-respect, honoring the divine within you.
2. **Using Faith to Reframe Negative Experiences**: Your spiritual beliefs can offer new perspectives on your experiences. Perhaps you see challenges as opportunities for growth or as tests of faith.

3. **Finding Spiritual Meaning in Personal Growth and Challenges**: View your healing journey as a spiritual journey as well. Each step forward in healing can be seen as a step closer to your higher purpose or true self.
4. **Developing a Personal Mantra or Affirmation Based on Faith**: Create a short, meaningful phrase based on your spiritual beliefs to repeat during difficult moments. For example: "I am worthy of love and respect, as a child of God."

Balancing Faith and Action

While faith can provide comfort and strength, it's important to balance spiritual support with practical action:

1. **Understanding the Importance of Both Spiritual Support and Practical Steps**: Recognize that healing requires both faith and effort on your part. Prayer and meditation can provide guidance and strength, but you must also take concrete steps to address the silent treatment in your relationship.
2. **Recognizing When to Seek Professional Help Alongside Spiritual Guidance**: Your faith leader or spiritual mentor can provide valuable support, but they may not be equipped to handle all aspects of emotional or psychological healing. Be open to seeking professional therapy or counseling when needed.

3. **Using Faith to Motivate Positive Changes in Your Life**: Let your spiritual beliefs inspire you to make positive changes. This might include setting healthy boundaries, practicing self-care, or working on your communication skills.

Overcoming Faith-Based Challenges

Your spiritual journey may not always be smooth. Here are some common challenges and how to address them:

1. **Addressing Feelings of Abandonment or Anger Towards a Higher Power**: It's normal to question your faith or feel angry at God or your higher power when going through difficult times. Allow yourself to express these feelings honestly in prayer or journaling.
2. **Navigating Conflicting Religious Views in Relationships**: If you and your partner have different religious beliefs, this can add complexity to addressing silent treatment. Seek guidance from interfaith counselors or spiritual leaders experienced in navigating these differences.
3. **Dealing with Spiritual Doubts That May Arise During Difficult Times**: Doubts are a normal part of any faith journey. Use this time to deepen your understanding of your beliefs. Remember that questioning can lead to stronger faith.

Faith and Self-Worth

Your spiritual beliefs can be a powerful tool in rebuilding your self-esteem:

1. **Understanding Your Inherent Value Through a Spiritual Lens:** Many faith traditions teach that each person has inherent worth as a creation of the divine. Reflect on what your faith says about your value as an individual.
2. **Using Faith to Combat Negative Self-Talk and Low Self-Esteem:** When you catch yourself in negative self-talk, counter it with affirming spiritual truths about your worth and lovability.
3. **Finding Strength in Spiritual Teachings About Love and Self-Compassion:** Explore your faith's teachings on self-love and compassion. Practice treating yourself with the same kindness and understanding that your faith encourages you to show others.

Sharing Your Faith Journey

Your spiritual growth can have a positive impact beyond your own healing:

1. **The Benefits of Connecting with Others Who Share Your Beliefs:** Seek out faith-based support groups or online communities where you can share your experiences and learn from others.
2. **How to Respectfully Discuss Your Faith with Non-Believers or Those of Different Faiths:**

Be open about how your faith has helped you, but respect others' beliefs or lack thereof. Focus on sharing your personal experience rather than trying to convert others.
3. **Using Your Experiences to Support Others in Their Spiritual Journey:** As you heal, you may find opportunities to support others facing similar challenges. Sharing your story can offer hope and guidance to those still struggling.

Faith and Future Relationships

Your spiritual beliefs can guide you in building healthier relationships:

1. **The Role of Shared Spiritual Values in Healthy Partnerships:** Consider the importance of shared or compatible spiritual beliefs in future relationships. While differences can be navigated, shared values can provide a strong foundation.
2. **Setting Faith-Based Boundaries in Relationships**: Use your spiritual beliefs to inform the boundaries you set in relationships. This might include expectations for communication, respect, and mutual support.
3. **Using Faith as a Guide for Future Relationship Choices:** Let your faith guide you in choosing partners who will respect you and support your spiritual growth.

Personal Stories of Faith and Healing

To conclude this chapter, I'd like to share a few brief stories from some friends who found strength through faith while dealing with silent treatment. These stories represent diverse spiritual backgrounds and experiences:

Story 1: Maria's Prayer for Peace

Maria, deeply rooted in her Catholic faith, felt the sting of silence from her close friend after a misunderstanding. The unspoken words hung heavy in the air, leaving her heart aching. Lost and alone, Maria turned to the familiar comfort of her faith. Each night, she knelt by her bed, her prayers a plea for strength, patience, and guidance. One particularly difficult night, she found solace in the rhythmic beads of the rosary, meditating on the mysteries of Christ's life. Over time, prayer became her anchor, and she began to realize that reconciliation, whether or not it came from her friend, had to first bloom within her own heart. The quiet moments of prayer brought a sense of calm, and eventually, the silence between her and her friend began to thaw, paving the way for healing and understanding.

Story 2: Ibrahim's Patience and the Quran's Wisdom

Ibrahim, a devout Muslim, found himself on the receiving end of the silent treatment from his brother, hurt by a decision Ibrahim had made. The silence created a painful rift in their family. Struggling to cope, Ibrahim turned to his faith for guidance. The teachings of the Prophet

Muhammad echoed in his mind, reminding him of the virtues of patience and the importance of family bonds. He began to recite verses from the Quran, words that spoke of patience and the strength to maintain family ties, even in the face of adversity. Through his daily prayers and reflection, Ibrahim found the strength to remain patient, resisting the urge to react in anger or frustration. He also sought forgiveness from Allah, asking for wisdom to navigate the situation with compassion. Over time, his patience bore fruit, and his brother reached out, ready to mend their relationship. Ibrahim learned a powerful lesson: faith and patience can bridge even the deepest divides.

Story 3: Priya's Meditation and the Path to Inner Peace

Priya, following the Hindu tradition, experienced the silent treatment from her spouse after a heated argument. The silence in their home was deafening, leaving Priya feeling deeply isolated. Seeking solace, she turned to her spiritual practices. Priya dedicated more time to meditation and chanting, her voice a gentle hum as she focused on mantras that invoked peace and understanding, like the sacred Gayatri Mantra. Through these practices, a sense of inner peace and clarity began to blossom within her. Her meditation sessions became a space for reflection, allowing her to see her own actions and understand her spouse's perspective. This newfound clarity led her to approach her spouse with compassion rather than defensiveness. The silence eventually gave way to open communication, and they were able to reconcile, their shared spiritual journey deepening their connection.

As a Christian, I've experienced the silent treatment firsthand, and it left me feeling abandoned, worthless, and questioning my own value. In those dark moments, I turned to my faith for strength and guidance. I found solace in reading scriptures that reminded me of God's unconditional love and my inherent worth as His child. I poured out my heart in prayer, seeking comfort and understanding. Through worship music, I found a way to express my emotions and connect with a community of believers.

My faith didn't magically erase the pain, but it provided a framework for healing. It reminded me that I wasn't alone, that even in silence God was with me. It gave me hope that even though the situation might not change, I could find peace and strength within myself. My faith journey taught me the importance of forgiveness, not just for the person who inflicted the silent treatment, but also for myself. It helped me see the experience as an opportunity for growth and develop greater compassion for others.

These stories demonstrate how individuals from different faith traditions—Christianity, Catholicism, Islam, and Hinduism—have found strength and healing through their spiritual practices when faced with the emotional challenge of the silent treatment. Each story reflects the universal power of faith to guide and support us through difficult times.

Remember, your spiritual journey is unique to you. As you navigate the challenges of healing from silent treatment, may your faith provide you with comfort, strength, and guidance. Trust your spiritual path, but also remain open to growth and new understandings. Your faith, like you, can emerge from this experience stronger and more resilient than ever.

With these spiritual tools added to our healing toolkit, we're ready to take on one of the most challenging yet rewarding aspects of recovery: reclaiming our love life. The next chapter will guide you through rebuilding healthy romantic relationships, whether you're working on your current partnership or considering future ones."

CHAPTER 8

RECLAIMING YOUR LOVE LIFE

After experiencing the silent treatment in a relationship, reclaiming your love life can feel like an insurmountable challenge. I remember standing in front of my closet, staring at clothes I hadn't worn in years, preparing for my first date after leaving my emotionally abusive relationship. My hands shook as I reached for a bright red blouse I loved.

"When was the last time I wore color?" I wondered aloud. The realization hit me hard - I had dimmed my own light for so long, trying to avoid triggering another bout of silence from my ex-partner. As I slipped on the blouse, I felt a mix of excitement and terror. Could I really do this? Was I ready to be seen again?

That moment in front of the mirror was the beginning of my journey to reclaim not just my love life, but my sense of self. It wasn't easy, and there were many moments of doubt along the way. But each step, each date (good or bad), and each moment of vulnerability brought me closer to the vibrant, confident woman I used to be - and beyond.

Understanding the Impact

The silent treatment leaves invisible scars. It erodes the trust and intimacy that healthy relationships are built upon. You might find yourself hesitant to open up, fearing that vulnerability will lead to more pain. Recognize that these feelings are normal responses to the emotional trauma you've experienced.

I remember how, even months after leaving my relationship, I'd flinch at certain phrases or tones of voice that reminded me of the silence. Understanding that these reactions were my mind's way of protecting me helped me approach healing with patience and self-compassion.

Take time to reflect on patterns in your past relationship. Were there specific triggers that led to silent treatment? How did you typically respond to the silence? Were there any of your own behaviors that may have contributed to communication breakdowns? This isn't about blaming yourself, but about gaining insight to make healthier choices moving forward.

Finding Your Worth

Silent treatment can leave you feeling worthless and undeserving of love. Rebuilding your self-esteem is crucial. Start by challenging negative self-talk. When you catch yourself thinking, "I'm not worthy of love," counter it with evidence of your worth.

Create a 'self-worth journal'. Each day, write down one thing you like about yourself or an accomplishment you're proud of. It might feel forced at first, but over time, you'll find it easier to recognize your value.

Remember, you are not inadequate because someone chose to use silence as a weapon. Their behavior reflects them, not you. Practice positive affirmations. Stand in front of a mirror and say, "I am worthy of respect and open communication." It might feel uncomfortable initially, but persevere.

Prioritize self-care and personal growth. Make time for activities that nourish your soul and help you grow. This could be anything from reading self-help books to taking up a new hobby or returning to an old passion.

I rediscovered my love for painting during my healing journey. Each stroke of the brush felt like reclaiming a part of myself that had been silenced. Find what lights you up and make it a non-negotiable part of your routine.

Communicating Your Needs

Clear boundaries are the cornerstone of healthy relationships. Reflect on what you need to feel safe and respected in a relationship. Write these down and commit to upholding them.

Learning to communicate assertively is a powerful tool. Practice using "I" statements to express your feelings and needs without blaming or attacking. For instance, instead of saying "You never listen to me," try "I feel unheard when my concerns are dismissed. I need to know that my feelings matter to you."

It's normal to feel anxious about expressing your needs after experiencing silent treatment. Start small. Practice expressing minor preferences or needs with friends or family. As you build confidence, you'll find it easier to advocate for yourself in romantic relationships.

Trust and Vulnerability

Trust is the bedrock of any healthy relationship. Understand that it's okay to be cautious about trusting again, but also recognize that not everyone will treat you the way your past partner did.

Rebuilding trust takes time. Start by trusting yourself and your judgment. As you enter new relationships, allow trust to build gradually. Find consistency between words and actions.

Vulnerability can feel scary after being hurt, but it's essential for genuine connection. Start by sharing small things about yourself and gradually work up to deeper disclosures as you feel safe. Remember, vulnerability is courage. It's not about winning or losing; it's about showing up and letting yourself be seen.

Dating After the Silent Treatment

As you re-enter the dating world, you do so with new wisdom. Trust your instincts. If something feels off, it probably is. At the same time, be open to the possibility of healthy connections.

Communicate your boundaries early in new relationships. It might feel uncomfortable, but the right person will respect your needs. Remember, you're not just looking for any relationship; you're looking for a healthy one.

Stay alert to signs of unhealthy communication patterns. If you notice a potential partner using silence as a weapon or avoiding difficult conversations, address it immediately. If the behavior persists, don't hesitate to walk away.

Finding a Supportive Partner

Seek a partner who values open communication, respects boundaries, and is emotionally available. Look for someone who takes responsibility for their actions and is willing to work through conflicts respectfully.

While chemistry is important, shared values and life goals are crucial for long-term compatibility. Take time to understand what truly matters to you in a relationship and look for a partner whose values align with yours.

A strong relationship is built on mutual respect, trust, and open communication. Take things slow, allowing time to build a solid foundation. Remember, a healthy relationship should add to your life, not complete it.

Reclaiming your love life after experiencing silent treatment is a journey. Be patient with yourself, celebrate your progress, and remember that you deserve a love that speaks, not one that stays silent. Your voice matters, and the right partner will not only listen but will also cherish what you have to say.

My Journey: Finding Love After Silent Treatment

After enduring a relationship where silent treatment was a constant, painful presence, I found myself at a crossroads. I knew I deserved better, but the prospect of opening my heart again was daunting. However, life had a surprise for me.

I remember our first date clearly. I wore my favorite red blouse, a choice that felt brave and vulnerable. While it wasn't perfect - we were both nervous and a bit awkward - there was an undeniable connection. His genuine interest in hearing my thoughts and feelings was refreshing and, honestly, a bit unfamiliar.

As we continued dating, I noticed how different this relationship felt. My previous experiences have taught me valuable lessons about self-worth and the importance of open communication. I was determined not to lose myself again, and I found myself naturally setting boundaries and expressing my needs more freely.

However, our journey wasn't without its challenges. My partner, I learned, was dealing with PTSD from previous experiences. There were times when his symptoms would flare up, causing him to withdraw or struggle with communication. In these moments, I felt echoes of my past relationship, triggering old fears and insecurities.

The difference this time was our shared commitment to growth and healing. My partner recognized the impact of his PTSD and took the courageous step of seeking counseling. Seeing his dedication to addressing his issues head-on gave me hope and strengthened my resolve to work on our relationship.

I, too, continued with individual counseling. My therapist helped me process my past experiences and develop healthier communication patterns. We worked on strategies to manage my triggers and build self-confidence.

Together, we also attended couples counseling. These sessions were invaluable in helping us understand each other better and develop tools for navigating difficult moments. We learned how to support each other during PTSD flare-ups without falling into patterns of silence or withdrawal.

Over time, our communication improved significantly. We developed a shared language for expressing our needs and fears. When silence did occur, it was no longer a weapon but a mutually understood need for space, always followed by open discussion.

Today, we're married, and our relationship continues to grow stronger. It's not perfect - we still face challenges and occasionally stumble. However, we face these moments together, with honesty and respect. The eggshell feeling that once dominated my life has faded, replaced by a sense of security and partnership.

My partner's ongoing commitment to his mental health, through continued counseling and self-work, has been crucial to our success. It's shown me that with the right person, love can be a journey of mutual growth and support.

Reflecting on that first date in my red blouse, I'm amazed at how far we've both come. Each step of this journey, even the difficult ones, has led us to where we are today - in a marriage built on understanding, open communication, and love.

For those who have experienced the pain of silent treatment, I want you to know that healing is possible. Whether it's in a new relationship or through personal growth, you can find your voice again. It takes time, effort, and often professional help. You deserve a love that hears you, respects you, and cherishes your voice.

Remember, your past experiences don't define you, but they can inform your growth. Trust your worth and the power of open, honest communication. The journey might not be easy, but it's absolutely worth it.

"As you work on rebuilding healthy relationships, you may encounter situations that make you question whether your current relationship can truly meet your needs. In the next chapter, we'll explore how to recognize when silence becomes truly detrimental and how to navigate this critical juncture in your journey."

CHAPTER 9

"WHEN SILENCE BECOMES DEAFENING: RECOGNIZING THE POINT OF NO RETURN"

Throughout this book, we've focused on understanding silent treatment, its impact, and strategies for addressing it within your relationship. We've explored healing, growth, and the possibility of positive change. However, it's crucial to recognize that sometimes the healthiest choice may be to leave the relationship. This chapter isn't about giving up but honoring yourself and your well-being.

In the following pages, we'll discuss recognizing when silent treatment has become too damaging to continue the relationship. We'll explore the signs that indicate it might be time to leave, how to make this difficult decision, and steps to take if you choose to end the relationship. Remember, considering leaving doesn't mean you've failed. Sometimes, it's the bravest and most self-loving choice you can make.

Let's navigate this challenging terrain together, with compassion for ourselves and a commitment to our well-being and happiness.

Anna's Story: The Moment of Truth

Anna, a close friend whose story profoundly resonates with many who've experienced silent treatment, shared her journey with me. Her experience illustrates the complex emotions and realizations that often accompany the decision to leave a relationship marred by chronic silent treatment.

Anna recalled the pivotal moment in her relationship:

"I remember standing in my home office, staring at a wall full of family photos. These were snapshots of happier times - holidays, birthdays, casual weekends. In each photo, I saw myself smiling, genuinely happy. But as I stood there, I realized I couldn't remember the last time I'd felt that way. The constant stress of navigating my partner's silence had drained not just my energy but my joy.

I picked up a recent photo of myself and barely recognized the woman staring back at me. My eyes looked tired, my smile forced. That's when it hit me—something had to change—not for the sake of our relationship but for my well-being and sanity.

I'd spent years trying to fix things, walking on eggshells, and blaming myself for the silence. But at that moment, looking at the stark contrast between my past and present self, I understood that I was losing myself while trying to save a relationship that was hurting me."

Recognizing the Danger Signs

Anna's experience highlighted some common indicators that silent treatment had crossed a line from a communication issue to emotional abuse:

- Frequency and Duration: "At first," Anna explained, "the silent episodes were infrequent and short-lived. But over time, they became more common and lasted longer. There were weeks when we barely exchanged more than a few words. The silence became suffocating."
- Impact on Self-esteem: Anna found herself constantly questioning her worth. "I started to believe that if I were just better - smarter, prettier, more interesting - maybe he would want to talk to me. I lost sight of my value outside of his approval."
- Isolation: The silent treatment caused Anna to withdraw from friends and activities she loved. "I stopped making plans with friends because I never knew what mood he'd be in. I was embarrassed to explain why I always canceled last minute. Eventually, it was easier just to stay home."
- Physical Symptoms: The stress began to manifest physically. "I developed insomnia," Anna shared. "I'd lie awake at night, replaying conversations in my head, trying to figure out what I'd done wrong.

I was constantly sick with colds and headaches. My body was telling me what my mind couldn't accept yet - that this situation was toxic."

- Loss of Self: Perhaps most alarmingly, Anna no longer recognized herself or felt connected to her passions. "I used to love painting but couldn't remember when I'd picked up a brush. My opinions, hobbies, and dreams seemed to fade away in the face of his silence."

Assessing Your Relationship

At this crossroads, Anna realized it was crucial to assess her relationship honestly. She asked herself several vital questions:

- Do I feel respected and valued in this relationship most of the time? Anna's answer: "No. The silence made me feel invisible and unimportant."
- Can I express my thoughts and feelings without fear of punishment through silence?Anna's answer: No! "I realized I was constantly censoring myself, afraid that saying the wrong thing would trigger another bout of silence."
- Is my partner willing to work on our communication issues? "I had brought up the issue multiple times, but he always dismissed my concerns or turned it back on me."
- Do I feel like my authentic self in this relationship? Anna's answer "No!"I felt like a shell of my

former self. I had lost touch with the vibrant, confident woman I used to be."

- Can I envision a future where we've overcome this issue? "Try as I might, I couldn't picture a future where this problem was resolved. The pattern seemed too deeply ingrained."

Anna's answers to these questions provided valuable insight into the health of her relationship and ultimately guided her decision to leave.

The Strength of Choosing to Leave

Choosing to leave a relationship marred by chronic silent treatment takes immense courage. It's not giving up—it's choosing yourself and your well-being.

Anna shared, "Deciding to leave was the hardest thing I've ever done. There was guilt, fear, and doubt. But it was also the most empowering choice I've ever made. I could hear my voice again for the first time in years."

The process was challenging for Anna. She described the steps she took:

1. ***Reaching out for support:*** "I confided in my sister and a close friend. Their support was crucial in giving me the strength to follow through with my decision."
2. ***Seeking professional help:*** "I started seeing a therapist who helped me navigate the complex emotions I was experiencing and supported me through the transition."

3. ***Creating a safety plan:*** "While my partner had never been physically abusive, I was concerned about how he might react. I ensured I had a safe place to go, and everyone knew my whereabouts during the separation process."
4. ***Focusing on healing:*** "I reminded myself daily that I deserved love and respect. I started to reconnect with old friends and rediscover my passions. It was like waking up after a long sleep."

Anna emphasized, "It's important to remember that healing is possible, and you deserve a life free from emotional abuse. Leaving doesn't mean you've failed - you're brave enough to choose yourself."

When Staying Might Be an Option

While Anna's story illustrates a situation where leaving was the best choice, it's important to acknowledge that in some cases, relationships can improve if both partners are committed to change.

This typically requires:

1. Both partners fully recognize the problem.
2. Commitment to change from both individuals.
3. Professional help, like couples therapy.
4. Clear boundaries and consequences for silent treatment.
5. Regular reassessment of progress.

However, Anna stressed the importance of prioritizing your safety and well-being. "If you choose to stay and work on the relationship, make sure it's because you see real potential for change, not out of fear or a misplaced sense of obligation."

Moving Forward

Whether you choose to stay and work on the relationship or leave to prioritize your well-being, know that you have the strength within you to create a life free from the pain of silent treatment.

In Anna's case, choosing to leave was the first step in reclaiming her voice and joy. She reflected, "It wasn't easy, and there were moments of doubt. But with time, I rediscovered parts of myself that had been silenced for so long. I started to see the smile in those old photos returning to my face."

Anna's journey didn't end with leaving. She continued to work on herself, rebuild her confidence, and create a life filled with open communication and mutual respect. "Now, when I look in the mirror, I see a woman who knows her worth. I'm painting again, laughing with friends, and looking forward to the future. Most importantly, I've learned never to let anyone silence me again." Anna stated!

Remember, your voice deserves to be heard, your feelings matter, and you are worthy of a relationship built on mutual respect, open communication, and love.

As we close this chapter, I want you to know that whatever you decide, it's okay. Trust yourself. You have the wisdom within you to make the right choice for your situation. And remember, choosing yourself is never selfish—it's necessary.

"Whether you've decided to stay and work on your relationship or to leave, recognizing the point where silence becomes unbearable is a crucial step. This realization opens the door to new possibilities and growth. In the next chapter, we'll explore how to move forward, regardless of your decision, and begin the process of long-term healing."

CHAPTER 10

"MOVING FORWARD: NAVIGATING YOUR PATH TO LONG-TERM HEALING"

As we continue our journey of healing and growth, it's time to explore advanced strategies for long-term recovery and navigate the path forward after addressing silent treatment. This chapter will guide you through personal growth, self-reflection, and making crucial decisions about your future.

Personal Growth and Self-Reflection

Addressing silent treatment in your relationship isn't just about improving communication—it's a profound journey of personal growth. As you work through this challenge, you may find yourself changing in unexpected and transformative ways.

I noticed that I became more assertive in other areas of my life. The skills I learned in expressing my needs to my partner translated into more confident interactions at work and with friends. I found myself speaking up in meetings, setting clear boundaries with family members, and even negotiating a raise at work—things I would have shied away from before.

I also developed a deeper sense of self-awareness. I began to catch myself before reacting negatively to situations, often pausing to ask, "Why am I feeling this way?" This introspection led to more thoughtful responses and fewer conflicts in all my relationships.

Perhaps most significantly, I discovered a wellspring of inner strength I didn't know I possessed. Confronting the silent treatment required courage, perseverance, and self-love. Recognizing these qualities in myself boosted my self-esteem and resilience.

Take time to reflect on how you've grown:

- Keep a growth journal. Each week, write down one way you've noticed yourself changing or a new strength you've discovered.
- Practice daily self-reflection. Spend 5-10 minutes each evening thinking about your daily interactions and responses.
- Ask trusted friends if they've observed differences in your behavior. Their outside perspective can often illuminate changes we might miss.
- Consider how your values or life goals may have shifted. Have new priorities or aspirations emerged through this process?

- Reflect on your emotional responses. Are you handling stress differently? Has your emotional regulation improved?

Remember, this growth is valuable regardless of your relationship's outcome. It's a part of you that you'll carry forward into all aspects of your life. Celebrate these changes—they're a testament to your resilience and capacity for growth.

Advanced Healing Strategies

As you continue your journey of healing and growth, it's time to delve into some more advanced strategies. These techniques have been instrumental in my ongoing recovery and may be helpful to you.

1. Rewriting Your Narrative

Silent treatment can make you the villain in your own story. It's time to pick up the pen and rewrite that narrative.

I started by literally rewriting my story. I took out my favorite journal and began writing about my experiences but with a twist. Instead of focusing on the pain of silent treatment, I wrote about my strength in facing it. I became the hero of my story, not the victim.

For instance, I wrote: "Despite the silence that threatened to drown her, she found her voice in the rustling pages of her books and the squeak of balloon rubber. Each word written, each book bound, each balloon twisted was an act of rebellion against the silence."

This exercise helped me see my experiences in a new light. It wasn't about denying the pain but about recognizing my resilience in the face of it.

To practice this:

- Choose a challenging experience related to silent treatment.
- Write about it from the perspective of a hero overcoming challenges.
- Focus on your strengths, wisdom gained, and personal growth.
- Read your story often, especially during difficult times, to remind yourself of your resilience.

2. Practicing Radical Acceptance

This advanced mindfulness technique involves fully accepting your reality, including the painful parts, without resistance.

This meant acknowledging: "Yes, I'm experiencing silent treatment. Yes, it hurts. And yes, I can handle this pain without letting it define me."

It doesn't mean you approve of the silent treatment; you'll tolerate it forever. It simply means you stop fighting against the reality of your current situation, which frees up energy to focus on your response to it.

I found it helpful to create a small 'acceptance' ritual. Whenever I noticed myself fighting against reality, I'd take a deep breath and craft a tiny origami book. The act of folding the paper became a physical representation of accepting and folding my experience into the larger story of my life. For a deeper approach, "I often find strength in the serenity prayer, asking for the wisdom to accept the things I cannot change, the courage to change the things I can, and the wisdom to know the difference. This prayer aligns perfectly with the practice of radical acceptance."

To incorporate radical acceptance:

- Notice when you're resisting your reality.
- Take a deep breath and say, "It is what it is at this moment."
- Find a physical action (like my origami) that represents acceptance for you.
- Accepting reality doesn't mean approving it or giving up on change.

3. Cultivating Self-Compassion

Self-compassion goes beyond self-esteem. It's about treating yourself with the same kindness you'd offer a good friend.

When I'm facing silent treatment, I place a hand over my heart and say, "This is a moment of suffering. Suffering is part of life. May I be kind to myself at this moment?" I remind myself that showing compassion to myself is also an act of honoring the divine spark within me. This perspective helps me treat myself with the kindness I'd offer to a loved one.

I've also incorporated self-compassion into my creative practices. When I make a mistake in my writing or bookbinding, instead of criticizing myself, I pause and say, "Everyone makes mistakes. This is an opportunity to learn and grow."

To practice self-compassion:

- Notice your self-talk. When it's harsh, pause.
- Ask yourself, "What would I say to a friend in this situation?"
- Offer those kind words to yourself.
- Include physical touch, like a hand on your heart, to reinforce self-compassion.

4. Embracing Imperfection

Perfectionism often goes hand-in-hand with the anxiety caused by silent treatment. Learning to embrace imperfection can be liberating.

I incorporated 'imperfect' elements, such as asymmetrical designs or unconventional color combinations, in my balloon art. These became my favorite pieces, reminding me that beauty often lies in imperfection.

I also applied this to my communication. Instead of striving for a 'perfect' response to silent treatment, I focused on authentic expression, whether messy or imperfect.

To embrace imperfection:

- Set 'imperfection goals.' Deliberately make small, harmless mistakes and sit with discomfort.
- Celebrate the unique aspects of your 'imperfect' creations or communications.
- Practice saying "good enough" instead of striving for perfection.
- Remind yourself that imperfections make you human and relatable.

5. Developing a Future Vision

While being present is important, having a vision for your future can provide hope and direction.

I created a 'vision book' – a book filled with words and images representing my ideal future. It included personal and relational aspirations. Part of my vision includes growing in my faith and using my experiences to help others, as I believe we're called to do. This adds a deeper sense of purpose to my healing journey. This book became a touchstone, reminding me of what I'm working towards.

Importantly, this vision was about me and my growth, not dependent on anyone else's behavior or the outcome of any particular relationship.

To create your future vision:

- Reflect on your values and what truly matters to you.

- Visualize your ideal life five years from now. What does it look like?
- Create a tangible representation – a vision board, a handmade book, or a series of sketches.
- Regularly revisit and refine your vision as you grow and change.

6. Mindfulness and Grounding Techniques

When silent treatment leaves you feeling adrift, mindfulness and grounding techniques can help you stay anchored in the present.

I developed a grounding routine using my senses. I'd find:

- Five things I could see (often focusing on my art supplies or books)
- Four things I could touch (feeling the texture of paper or balloon rubber)
- Three things I could hear (maybe the rustle of pages or the squeak of balloons)
- Two things I could smell (ink, perhaps, or the scent of a scented candle in my workspace)
- One thing I could taste (often a sip of tea)

This practice helped bring me back to the present moment when anxiety about the silent treatment threatened to overwhelm me.

To practice grounding:

- Develop your own sensory routine.
- Practice it regularly, not just during stressful times.

- Incorporate elements of your passions or creative pursuits for added comfort.
- Use this technique as a bridge to more extended mindfulness practices.

7. Deciding Your Path Forward

After putting in the work to address silent treatment, you may reach a crossroads. Some couples find their bond strengthened, while others realize they've grown apart. Both outcomes are valid, and the decision to move forward is deeply personal and often complex.

In my case, addressing silent treatment revealed fundamental incompatibilities we hadn't previously acknowledged. It was a painful realization but an important one for both of us. We found that while our communication had improved, our core values and life goals had diverged over time.

As you stand at this crossroads, consider these paths:

Staying and continuing to build a stronger relationship: If you've seen significant positive changes and feel a renewed commitment to each other, this might be your path. It requires ongoing work but can lead to a deeply fulfilling relationship.

- Regularly check in on your progress
- Continue to practice and refine your communication skills
- Be prepared for occasional setbacks, viewing them as opportunities for further growth

- Celebrate your improvements and the new strength of your bond

Choosing to separate and focusing on individual healing: Sometimes, addressing silent treatment reveals that the relationship has run its course. Separation might be the healthiest choice if your personal growth is leading you in different directions.

- Allow yourself to grieve the end of the relationship
- Focus on your individual goals and aspirations
- Continue to apply the communication skills you've learned in other relationships
- Seek support from friends, family, or a therapist during this transition

"Conscious uncoupling" - a collaborative, respectful parting: This approach, popularized in recent years, involves working together to end the romantic relationship while maintaining respect and care for each other.

- Commit to open, honest communication throughout the separation process
- Work together to address practical matters (like shared finances or living arrangements) with fairness and consideration
- If children are involved, prioritize their well-being and commit to positive co-parenting

- Acknowledge the good in your relationship even as you choose to end it

Whichever path you choose, make the decision from a place of self-awareness and honesty, not fear or habit. Take your time with this decision—there's no rush. You might find it helpful to write out each option's pros and cons or discuss your thoughts with a trusted friend or therapist.

Remember, there's no "right" or "wrong" decision here. The best choice is the one that aligns with your authentic self and allows both you and your partner the best opportunity for happiness and growth.

8. Self-Care and Support

Regardless of your decision, prioritizing self-care and seeking support is crucial. The emotional work of addressing silent treatment can be draining, and you need to replenish your reserves to maintain your mental and emotional health.

I had neglected many of my needs while focusing on the relationship. Reconnecting with old friends and rediscovering forgotten hobbies became essential to my healing process. I started taking yoga classes, which helped me manage stress and stay grounded. I also joined a book club, which provided intellectual stimulation and new social connections.

Ideas for self-care and support:

- Establish a daily self-care routine. This could include meditation, exercise, journaling, or any activity that nurtures your well-being.
- Prioritize sleep and nutrition. Emotional stress can take a physical toll, so taking care of your body is essential.
- Reconnect with friends and family. Don't hesitate to lean on your support network during this time.
- Consider joining a support group. Sharing experiences with others who understand can be incredibly healing.
- Seek therapy or counseling. A professional can provide valuable guidance and support as you navigate this transition.
- Engage in activities that bring you joy and relaxation. Rediscover old hobbies or explore new interests.
- Practice mindfulness. This can help you stay present and manage anxiety about the future.
- Set boundaries. Learn to say no to commitments that drain your energy.

Remember, taking care of yourself isn't selfish—it's necessary for your well-being and positively impacts all your relationships. Self-care is not a luxury but a fundamental aspect of healing and personal growth.

9. Looking to the Future

As you move forward, it's important to carry the lessons you've learned into the future, whether in your current relationship or new ones. This is a time to reimagine what you want your life to look like and set intentions for your future relationships.

I took time to envision what I truly wanted in a relationship. This vision became a guidepost, helping me make decisions aligned with my values and needs. I realized I wanted a partnership built on open communication, mutual respect, and shared goals—things I now knew were non-negotiable for my happiness.

Steps for future planning:

- Write down your non-negotiables for a healthy relationship. What are the core values and behaviors you need in a partnership?
- Set personal goals independent of your relationship status. What do you want to achieve in your career, personal growth, or other areas of life?
- If staying together, create shared goals with your partner. How do you want your relationship to look in one year? Five years?
- If separating, focus on building a fulfilling single life. What new experiences do you want to have? What parts of yourself do you want to develop?
- Create a vision board or write a detailed description of your ideal future. Make it vivid and inspiring.

- Break your big goals into smaller, actionable steps. What can you do this week to move towards your vision?
- Regularly review and adjust your goals. Your vision for the future may evolve as you grow and change.

Remember, the future is full of possibilities. Though painful, your experience with silent treatment has equipped you with valuable insights for creating healthier relationships. You now have a clearer understanding of your needs, improved communication skills, and a stronger sense of self. These are powerful tools for building the future you desire.

10. Helping Others

Your journey through addressing silent treatment has given you a unique perspective that could be invaluable to others facing similar challenges. Sharing your experience can not only help others but can also be a powerful part of your own healing process.

After working through my experience, I naturally supported friends struggling with communication issues. Sharing my story gave others hope and practical strategies. One friend told me that hearing about my journey gave her the courage to address the silent treatment in her relationship.

Ways to help others:

- Share your story when appropriate. Be open about your experiences when the opportunity arises.
- Offer a listening ear to friends in need. Sometimes, people just need to know they're not alone.
- Consider volunteering with relationship support organizations. Your firsthand experience could be incredibly valuable.
- Write about your experiences. This could be in a blog, support forum, or even a book like this.
- Become a peer support mentor. Some organizations offer training for people who want to support others going through similar experiences.
- Organize a support group in your community. Create a safe space for people to share and learn from each other.
- Advocate for healthy relationship education. Consider speaking at schools or community centers about the importance of healthy communication.

By helping others, you reinforce your own healing and growth. Turning a painful experience into a source of support for others can be incredibly empowering. However, remember to maintain healthy boundaries and ensure you're in a good place emotionally before supporting others.

Remember, moving forward after addressing silent treatment is a personal journey. There's no one-size-fits-all solution. Trust yourself, be patient with the process, and know that you have the strength to create a future filled with healthy, open communication—whether in your current relationship or new connections you'll form.

Your experience has given you valuable tools for building stronger, more authentic relationships in all areas of your life. You've survived a challenging situation and grown and evolved through it. Carry this strength and wisdom with you as you move forward. Your future self will thank you for your hard work and the courage you've shown in addressing silent treatment and reclaiming your voice.

"Now that we've charted a path forward, it's time to focus on integrating these healing strategies into your daily life. The next chapter will provide practical ways to make these new habits and mindsets a permanent part of your journey."

CHAPTER 11

"LIVING YOUR BEST LIFE: INTEGRATING HEALING STRATEGIES INTO DAILY LIFE"

Now that we've explored some advanced strategies, let's talk about how to weave these practices into the fabric of your everyday life. Remember, healing isn't just about significant breakthroughs – it's about the small, consistent actions we take daily.

Creating a Daily Healing Routine

A structured daily practice helped anchor me, especially when silent treatment left me adrift. My practice combines the strategies we've discussed: "I often start my day with a moment of gratitude, thanking my God for another day and the strength to face its challenges. Being grateful sets a positive tone for my healing ."

After my prayers, I write one page in my journal—a practice called 'Morning Pages.' It's a stream-of-consciousness writing that helps clear my mind and often reveals insights I didn't know I had.

Then, I choose a small creative project – a quick sketch, a tiny handmade book, or a simple balloon sculpture. This act of creation reminds me of my capabilities and brings joy to the start of my day.

I end my routine with a moment of mindfulness, often using the grounding technique we discussed earlier.

This process takes about 30 minutes but sets a tone of self-care and intentionality for the entire day.

To develop your routine

- Choose elements that resonate with you. It could include journaling, art, meditation, affirmations, or gentle movement.
- Start small – even 5-10 minutes can make a difference.
- Be consistent. Do it at the same time each day if possible.
- Allow flexibility. If you miss a day, be kind to yourself and start again the next day.

Micro-Moments of Self-Compassion

While having a dedicated practice is valuable, sprinkling moments of self-compassion throughout your day is equally important. I call these 'micro-moments'.

For instance, when I feel the sting of silent treatment, I pause and take three deep breaths. With each exhale, I silently say, "I am worthy of love and respect." It takes just a few seconds but helps reset my emotional state.

Another micro-moment practice I use involves my art. Whenever I pass by my craft supplies, I pause to appreciate the colors, textures, and possibilities they represent. This moment of beauty and potential lifts my spirits, even on difficult days.

To incorporate micro-moments:

- Identify triggers that often lead to negative self-talk or anxiety.
- Create a list of quick, simple self-compassion practices.
- Practice your chosen micro-moment whenever you encounter a trigger.
- Celebrate each time you remember to be kind to yourself.

Weekly Check-Ins and Reflections

While daily practices are crucial, weekly reflections help me see the bigger picture of my healing journey.

Every Sunday evening, I sit down with my favorite pen and a journal I've made just for this purpose. "I reflect on moments where I felt a sense of peace or guidance, recognizing these as spiritual touchstones in my week. This helps me stay connected to my faith throughout my healing journey. "I reflect on the past week, asking myself:

- What challenges did I face? How did I handle them?
- What moments of strength or resilience am I proud of?
- How did I practice self-compassion this week?
- What did I learn about myself?
- What do I want to focus on next week?

This practice helps me recognize my progress, even when it feels slow. It also allows me to adjust my strategies as needed.

To start your weekly reflections

- Choose a consistent time and place.
- Create or choose a journal for this purpose.
- Start with the questions above, and add your own over time.
- Be honest, but also kind to yourself in your reflections.

Creating a Supportive Environment

Our environment plays a massive role in our healing process. I've intentionally shaped my living space to support my emotional well-being.

I've created a small 'inspiration corner' in my home. It's filled with my handmade books, favorite art supplies, and objects that bring me joy. When silent treatment makes me feel small, I can go to this corner and be reminded of my creativity and worth.

I've also placed small 'anchors' throughout my home—a beautiful stone on my nightstand, a framed affirmation on my desk, and a tiny potted plant in the kitchen. Each serves as a visual reminder to pause, breathe, and reconnect with myself.

To create a supportive environment

- Identify areas in your home where you spend the most time.
- Choose objects that represent strength, creativity, or peace to you.
- Place these 'anchors' strategically around your space.
- Regularly refresh or rotate these objects to keep their impact strong.

Balancing Solitude and Connection

Healing from the effects of silent treatment often requires finding a new balance between time alone and time with others.

I've learned to appreciate solitude as a time for self-reflection and creativity. My solo bookbinding sessions have become a form of meditation, allowing me to process my emotions while creating something beautiful.

At the same time, I've recognized the importance of meaningful connections. I've joined local writers' and balloon artists' groups. These communities provide support, inspiration, and a reminder that I'm not alone in my journey. "I've found that solitude and connection can be forms of communion - with myself, others, and something greater than myself. This perspective helps me find meaning in my alone time and interactions with others."

To find your balance

- Schedule regular 'dates' with yourself for creative pursuits or self-reflection.
- Identify communities or groups aligned with your interests.
- Practice vulnerable sharing with trusted friends or a therapist.
- Notice how you feel after time alone vs. with others, and adjust as needed.

Remember, integrating these practices into your life is a process. There will be days when it feels effortless and a struggle. The key is to approach it all with patience and self-compassion. You're not just healing from silent treatment but building a richer, more authentic life—every small step matters. Keep going, keep creating, keep growing. Your journey is uniquely yours and beautiful in all its imperfect glory."

"As we integrate these strategies into our daily lives, it's important to remember that healing is a long-term process. The next chapter will explore how to sustain your progress and navigate the ongoing journey of recovery."

CHAPTER 12

"THE LONG HAUL: SUSTAINING YOUR HEALING JOURNEY"

Healing from silent treatment isn't a sprint; it's a marathon. In this section, we'll explore how to sustain your progress over the long term and navigate the inevitable ebbs and flows of the healing process.

Understanding the Healing Cycle

It's crucial to recognize that healing isn't linear. I've found it helpful to think of it as a spiral—you may revisit old issues, but each time you do, you approach them from a higher level of understanding and strength.

In my journey, there were times when I felt I was back at square one. A particularly hurtful episode of silent treatment would leave me feeling as vulnerable as I did at the beginning. But then I realized I was handling it differently - with more tools, self-awareness, and self-compassion. That's when I understood I was spiraling upward, not going in circles.

To embrace this cycle

- Keep a healing journal to track your progress over time
- Celebrate small victories, even when facing old challenges
- Remind yourself that revisiting issues doesn't mean regression

Adapting Your Strategies Over Time

What works for you now might not work well in six months or a year. I've learned to reassess my coping strategies and adjust them as needed periodically.

For example, while journaling was initially my go-to method for processing emotions, I later found that creating visual art became more effective. My handmade books evolved from simple journals to complex art pieces that expressed what I couldn't put into words.

To keep your strategies fresh

- Schedule quarterly "strategy check-ins" with yourself
- Be open to trying new healing modalities
- Pay attention to what energizes you versus what feels like a chore

Handling Triggers and Flashbacks

Even as you heal, you may encounter situations that trigger old wounds. Learning to manage these moments is crucial for long-term healing.

I remember the first time I encountered silent treatment in a new relationship after I'd done significant healing work. The familiar panic started to set in, but this time, I was prepared. I used grounding techniques, reached out to my support system, and reminded myself how far I'd come.

Strategies for managing triggers:

- Develop a "trigger action plan" in advance
- Practice mindfulness to catch triggers early
- Use positive self-talk to remind yourself of your strength

Maintaining Boundaries in the Long Term

Setting boundaries is one thing; maintaining them over time is another challenge entirely. It requires consistent effort and, sometimes, difficult conversations.

My resolve to maintain boundaries would sometimes waver, especially when things were going well. I had to remind myself that boundaries are not punishments but acts of self-care that contribute to healthier relationships.

Tips for long-term boundary maintenance:

- Regularly review and reaffirm your boundaries

- Prepare scripts for reinforcing boundaries when needed
- Celebrate moments when you successfully maintain a boundary

Evolving Your Support System

As you grow and change, your support needs may shift. Some relationships may no longer serve your healing journey, while new, supportive connections may form.

As I became stronger, I needed different things from my support system. Instead of just comfort, I started seeking accountability and growth-oriented support.

To evolve your support system:

- Periodically assess if your current support meets your needs
- Be open to forming new connections
- Don't be afraid to distance yourself from relationships that hinder your growth

Integrating Your Healing into Your Identity

Over time, your work becomes a part of who you are. This integration can be beautiful but challenging as you navigate your evolving sense of self.

This meant seeing myself not as a victim of silent treatment but as a survivor and thriver. My experiences and healing journey became part of my story, informing my art, relationships, and purpose.

To integrate healing into your identity:

- Reflect on how your experiences have shaped you positively
- Incorporate your healing journey into your narrative
- Use your growth as inspiration in your creative pursuits

Passing It On Using Your Experience to Help Others

Many find that sharing their journey and helping others is vital to their healing. This doesn't mean you must become a full-time advocate, but finding ways to support others can be deeply fulfilling.

I started by sharing my experiences through my art and writing. Later, I found myself mentoring others just beginning their healing journey. This not only helped them but also reinforced my growth.

Ways to pass on your experience:

- Share your story through art, writing, or speaking
- Offer support in online forums or support groups
- Consider volunteering with organizations that support abuse survivors

Nurturing Your Faith Throughout the Journey

Faith can be a powerful anchor throughout your healing journey. Nurturing this aspect of your life as you grow and heal is essential.

In my darkest moments, my faith reminded me that I was never truly alone. I found comfort in prayer and believing that my struggles had a purpose. As I healed, my relationship with my faith evolved, becoming a source of strength and guidance.

To nurture your faith:

- Incorporate spiritual practices into your daily routine
- Seek out faith-based support groups or counseling
- Allow your understanding of faith to grow with you

Remember, sustaining your healing journey involves commitment, flexibility, and self-compassion. There will be challenges along the way, but each is an opportunity for growth. Trust in the process, lean on your support system (including your faith if that's part of your journey), and keep moving forward. Your path to healing is uniquely yours, and every step you take is a victor.

"Rebuilding and Growing: Navigating the Emotional Landscape"

As you work to strengthen your relationship after years of silent treatment, you may encounter a range of challenging emotions. Resistance, distrust, numbness, and feeling stuck are everyday experiences. Let's explore these feelings and how to navigate them:

Confronting Resistance

Resistance to change can come from both partners. You might hesitate to hope for improvement, or your partner may be reluctant to abandon familiar patterns.

I remember feeling a knot in my stomach every time we tried to discuss our communication issues. Part of me wanted to cling to the familiar, even if it was painful. My partner often seemed to retreat into silence out of habit.

One particular evening stands out. We had agreed to have a 'communication date,' but as the time approached, I felt an overwhelming urge to cancel. I busied myself with meaningless tasks around the house as if I could clean away my fears. When my partner arrived, I saw the same hesitation in their eyes. We sat in uncomfortable silence for hours before I finally blurted out, "This is terrifying." Surprisingly, that vulnerability broke the ice, and we laughed nervously. It was a small step, showing me that pushing through resistance could lead to meaningful moments.

Strategies for Overcoming Resistance:

- Acknowledge the fear behind the resistance. Often, it's fear of the unknown or fear of failure.
- Take small, manageable steps rather than expecting immediate, dramatic change.
- Celebrate each small victory to build momentum and confidence.
- Consider writing letters to each other if verbal communication feels too daunting at first.

Rebuilding Trust

After years of silent treatment, trust can be severely damaged. You might find yourself constantly waiting for the other shoe to drop or struggling to believe that real change is possible.

There were days when my partner would try to communicate, but I'd find myself braced for the silence to return. It felt safer to expect disappointment than hope for lasting change.

I recall when my partner constantly checked in with me for a week, asking about my day and sharing their thoughts. Instead of feeling relieved, I found myself increasingly anxious. One night, I couldn't sleep, convinced that this positive change meant something terrible was about to happen. I confessed these fears to my partner by shaking hands the following day. Their understanding response was the first step in a long journey of rebuilding trust.

Strategies for Rebuilding Trust:

- Start with small, low-stakes promises and consistently keep them.
- Be patient with yourself and your partner. Trust takes time to rebuild.
- Practice transparency in your actions and decisions.
- Consider creating a 'trust journal' where you note positive interactions and keep promises.

Dealing with Emotional Numbness

Prolonged exposure to silent treatment can lead to a sense of emotional numbness. You might feel disconnected from your feelings or struggle to engage emotionally with your partner.

There was a period where I felt like I was going through the motions in our relationship. I'd grown so accustomed to the emotional distance that I struggled to reconnect, even when given the opportunity.

This numbness seeped into every aspect of my life. I went through my daily routine without any real engagement or joy. One day, a friend commented that I seemed "checked out." It was a wake-up call. I realized I had been operating on autopilot, not just in my relationship but in all aspects of my life. That night, I forced myself to sit down and think about how I truly felt, not just what I thought I should feel. It was like lancing a wound – painful, but the first step towards healing.

Strategies for Overcoming Numbness:

- Practice mindfulness to reconnect with your emotions. Try body scans or emotion check-ins throughout the day.
- Engage in expressive activities. For me, creating art or writing helped me tap into buried emotions.
- Seek individual therapy to work through emotional blockages.
- Gradually increase emotional intimacy through structured exercises like the '36 Questions That Lead to Love'.

Breaking Free from Feeling Stuck

The cycle of silent treatment can make you feel trapped, unsure of how to move forward or if change is even possible.

Sometimes, I felt like we were in relationship purgatory—not happy but unable to envision a different future. This inertia was almost as painful as the silent treatment itself.

I remember lying awake night after night, trapped in indecision and fear. Then, during a particularly frustrating moment, I started listing everything I wanted in a relationship, regardless of whether I thought they were possible. Before I knew it, I had created a vision of a relationship so different from what I had, and it was almost shocking. This exercise didn't magically fix things, but it gave me a new perspective and the energy to start making small changes.

Strategies for Unsticking:

- Envision your ideal relationship. What would healthy communication look like?
- Set clear, achievable goals for improving your relationship. Write them down and revisit them regularly.
- Consider a trial period of new communication habits. Commit to trying for a set time, then evaluate.
- Seek couples therapy for professional guidance in moving forward.

Cultivating Patience and Self-Compassion

Rebuilding a relationship after years of silent treatment is a long process. Being patient with yourself, your partner, and the process is crucial.

I often felt frustrated with myself for not healing faster or for still being affected by past hurts. Learning to be patient and kind to myself was crucial to the healing process.

There was a day when I completely lost my composure over a minor miscommunication with my partner. I berated myself for overreacting, feeling like I had undone months of progress. In my distress, I took a long walk. As I observed the slow, steady growth of trees and plants around me, I realized that healing works the same way – it's a gradual process, and every small effort matters, even if it doesn't feel significant. From that day on, I started to celebrate small victories and began treating myself with the same care and patience I would offer a dear friend.

Strategies for Patience and Self-Compassion:

- Practice daily self-compassion exercises. Speak to yourself as you would a dear friend.
- Keep a 'progress journal' to remind yourself how far you've come.
- Set realistic expectations for the pace of change.
- Regularly engage in self-care activities. These often involve creative pursuits like crafting a hand-bound book or creating art.

Remember, healing from years of silent treatment is not a linear process. There will be setbacks and difficult days. But building a healthier, more communicative relationship is possible with persistence, self-compassion, and a commitment to growth.

In my faith, I've found comfort in the idea of grace - giving grace to others and myself. This perspective has helped me navigate the challenging emotions of rebuilding a relationship.

As you work through these feelings, don't hesitate to seek support. Whether through therapy, support groups, or trusted friends, having a support system can make a significant difference in your healing journey."

"As we conclude our journey together, it's time to fully embrace your voice and the strength you've discovered. In our final chapter, we'll reflect on how far you've come and look ahead to a future where your voice is heard, respected, and valued."

CHAPTER 13

"EMBRACING YOUR VOICE: FINAL THOUGHTS AND ENCOURAGEMENT"

As we end this journey together, I want to acknowledge the courage and strength you've shown by confronting the issue of silent treatment in your relationship. Whether you picked up this book out of curiosity, desperation, or anywhere in between, you've taken a significant step towards healthier communication and a more fulfilling life.

Recap of the Journey

We've covered a lot of ground in these pages. We've explored the devastating impact of silent treatment, delved into the reasons behind this harmful behavior, and most importantly, discussed strategies for breaking the cycle. We've discussed setting boundaries, rebuilding trust, and rediscovering your voice.

Remember, addressing silent treatment isn't just about improving your relationship—it's about reclaiming your self-worth and asserting your right to be heard. The path isn't always easy, but it's incredibly worthwhile.

The Ongoing Nature of Growth

As you move forward from here, remember that personal growth and healing are ongoing processes. There's no finite endpoint where you can say, "I'm done growing now." And that's a beautiful thing! It means that every day brings new learning opportunities for strengthening your relationships and becoming more authentic.

Reflect on your experiences and emotions. Celebrate your progress, learn from your setbacks, and keep moving forward. The skills you've developed in addressing silent treatment—assertiveness, emotional awareness, and clear communication—will serve you well in all areas of your life.

Embracing Your Authentic Self

Through this process of addressing silent treatment, you've likely uncovered previously hidden or suppressed aspects of yourself. Perhaps you've rediscovered your passion for specific hobbies or realized you have stronger opinions than you thought. Maybe you've found a well of inner strength you didn't know existed.

Embrace these discoveries. With all its quirks, passions, and unique perspectives, your authentic self is worthy of expression and respect. Keep this authenticity as you move forward, whether in your current relationship or future ones. It's the foundation of genuine connection and fulfilling relationships.

The Ripple Effect of Healthy Communication

As you've worked on improving communication in your romantic relationship, you may have noticed changes in other areas of your life, too. You might be more assertive at work or open with friends and family. This positive change often extends to different aspects of your life.

By addressing silent treatment and committing to open, honest dialogue, you're not just changing your life—you're potentially influencing those around you. You're showing others what healthy communication looks like. You're breaking generational patterns of harmful behavior. Essentially, you're becoming an agent of positive change in your community.

A Message of Hope

To those who are still in the thick of it, still experiencing the pain and confusion of silent treatment, I want you to know this: there is hope. Change is possible. You have the strength to address this issue, heal, and create healthier relationships.

It may feel overwhelming now, but take it one step at a time. Start by recognizing your worth. You deserve to be heard and respected and have open and honest communication. Keep that truth, even when it's complicated.

Final Call to Action

As you close this book, I encourage you to commit—or recommit—to open, honest communication in all your relationships. You'll encounter challenges and make mistakes, but your commitment to trying, learning, and growing remains steadfast.

Here are some immediate steps you can take:

- Write a letter to yourself affirming your commitment to healthy communication
- Have an open conversation with a loved one about your communication goals
- Practice one new communication technique you've learned from this book
- Schedule some dedicated self-care time to reflect on your journey

Closing Thoughts

Writing this book has been a profound journey for me. Revisiting my own experiences with silent treatment wasn't always easy, but it reinforced for me the importance of this work. It reminded me of how far I've come and filled me with hope for all those on this path.

Remember, your voice matters, your feelings are valid, and your desire for open, respectful communication is not just reasonable—it's essential for your well-being and the health of your relationships.

As you move forward from here, be patient with yourself. Healing and growth take time. Setbacks may occur along the way, but don't let them discourage you. Every step forward, however small, is a victory.

You've already shown immense courage by confronting this issue. Carry that courage with you as you continue your journey. Trust your strength, believe in your worth, and never stop using your voice.

Thank you for allowing me to be a part of your journey. I believe in you, and I'm rooting for you every step of the way. Here's to healthier communication, more fulfilling relationships, and a future where your voice is heard, respected, and valued.

Remember, you are not alone in this journey. Your story of overcoming silent treatment could be the inspiration someone else needs. Share your experiences, support others, and advocate for healthy communication in all your relationships.

As you close this book, know that this isn't an ending but a new beginning. You have the power to write the next chapter of your life—one filled with open communication, mutual respect, and genuine connection. Your voice is your power. Use it, cherish it, and let it lead you towards the fulfilling relationships you deserve."

RESOURCES

Support Groups and Organizations for Survivors of Emotional Abuse

Disclaimer: While I provide a list of organizations, it's crucial to verify the information and contact details as contact information and services can change over time.

National and International Organizations

- **The National Domestic Violence Hotline:** 1-800-799-SAFE (7233) - Offers crisis intervention, safety planning, and referrals to local resources.
- **The National Sexual Assault Hotline:** 1-800-656-HOPE - While primarily focused on sexual assault, they can provide resources for survivors of all types of abuse.
- **The National Alliance on Mental Illness (NAMI):** 1-800-950-NAMI (6264) - Offers support and education on mental health conditions, including those related to abuse.
- **The Trevor Project:** 1-866-488-7386 - Provides crisis intervention and support for LGBTQ+ youth.
- **Childhelp USA:** 1-800-422-4453 - Dedicated to helping abused, neglected, and exploited children.

Additional Resources

- **Local Domestic Violence Shelters:** Contact your local government or social services for information on shelters in your area.
- **Mental Health Professionals:** Therapists and counselors can provide support and guidance for healing from emotional abuse.
- **Support Groups:** Online and in-person support groups offer a safe space for survivors to connect and share experiences.
- **Legal Aid Societies:** If you're facing legal issues related to abuse, legal aid societies can provide assistance.

General Support and Information Websites

The National Domestic Violence Hotline: Website: https://www.thehotline.org/

- **Psychology Today:** Offers articles and therapist directories.
    - Website: https://www.psychologytoday.com/
- **Verywell Mind:** Provides information on mental health and well-being.
    - Website: https://www.verywellmind.com/

Online Forums and Communities

- **Reddit:** Subreddits like r/relationships, r/domestic violence, and r/abuse can offer support and information.

- **Online Support Groups:** Search for online support groups focused on emotional abuse or narcissistic relationships.

www.ingramcontent.com/pod-product-compliance
Lightning Source LLC
Chambersburg PA
CBHW070852050426
42453CB00012B/2156